Think

Rem

ark

able

Think Remarkable

9 Paths to Transform Your Life and Make a Difference

GUY KAWASAKI

Foreword by
JANE GOODALL

with MADISUN NUISMER

WILEY

Published by John Wiley & Sons, Inc., Hoboken, New Jersey.
Published simultaneously in Canada.

For general information on our other products and services or for technical support, please contact our Customer Care Department within the United States at (800) 762-2974, outside the United States at (317) 572-3993 or fax (317) 572-4002.

Wiley also publishes its books in a variety of electronic formats. Some content that appears in print may not be available in electronic formats. For more information about Wiley products, visit our web site at www.wiley.com.

Library of Congress Cataloging-in-Publication Data:

Names: Kawasaki, Guy, 1954- author. | Nuismer, Madisun, author.
Title: Think remarkable : 9 paths to transform your life and make a difference / Guy Kawasaki and Madisun Nuismer.
Description: First edition. | Hoboken, New Jersey : Wiley, [2024] | Includes index.
Identifiers: LCCN 2023053754 (print) | LCCN 2023053755 (ebook) | ISBN 9781394245222 (cloth) | ISBN 9781394245246 (adobe pdf) | ISBN 9781394245239 (epub)
Subjects: LCSH: Self-perception. | Belief and doubt. | Motivation (Psychology) | Success—Psychological aspects. | Self-actualization (Psychology) | Courtesy.
Classification: LCC BF697.5.S43 K39 2024 (print) | LCC BF697.5.S43 (ebook) | DDC 158.1—dc23/eng/20231218
LC record available at https://lccn.loc.gov/2023053754
LC ebook record available at https://lccn.loc.gov/2023053755

Cover Design: Chris Wallace
Author Photos by Liz DePuydt
SKY10062737_010824

To Gen Z. Your time has come.

Contents

Foreword

When Guy asked me to write this foreword, my list of "to write" items was at twenty-one. I had just returned from Tanzania and Uganda. Before that, I was in Japan and South Korea. The next week I would be in Canada, the United States, and Brazil. And then I was due to be off to Spain and Switzerland, and finally back to LA.

So I really didn't have time. But Guy is a friend, and because this book provides guidance that will help people find a way of living their lives in a world of increasing uncertainty and complexity, I said yes.

In fact, in the time since I agreed to his request, the state of things has grown even worse and more people are becoming depressed because of changing weather patterns, loss of species, and the horror of war.

In *Think Remarkable,* Guy discusses three qualities—growth, grit, and grace—that can help us adapt and survive in these tumultuous times. And he explores ways we can move toward a world changed for the better.

Clearly **Growth**, in the sense of adapting to rapid change and coping with new, difficult, and often unforeseen challenges, is important. On a planet with finite natural resources (already running out in some places) and growing populations of humans and livestock, we must change the way we conduct business, the way we grow our food, and so on.

Think Remarkable argues that we must develop a new mindset: to survive in this rapidly changing world, we must push ourselves to grow mentally, to find new ways of living our day-to-day lives, and to develop technology that will help us live in greater harmony with nature. We must grow emotionally and ethically so that we can cope with problems such as poverty, racism, and discrimination.

And for us to develop this new mindset we must have **Grit**: we must be able to endure. As climate and weather patterns change, animals and plants that cannot adapt or move to more suitable environments will gradually become extinct. With our highly developed intellect, we can find ways of adapting, but only if we have grit, the courage to tackle what at first seems overwhelming.

We must have the courage of our convictions to stand up to corporations and governments that put short-term profit above protecting the environment for future generations. One of my own reasons for hope is the resilience of nature. And this book clearly explains the principles that can help us to cultivate resilience, empowering us to stand steadfast, stay true to our values even when we are up against overwhelming odds.

We must take lessons from the resilience of Mother Nature. As I travel around the world, I have seen so many places that were once almost entirely destroyed as a result of human activity, but where—when given time and perhaps some help—nature has returned and plants and animals have been given another chance.

We too must learn to "withstand the slings and arrows of outrageous fortune." And we must take courage from the amazing men and women who have accomplished what seems impossible and never given up despite being reviled or even imprisoned for their beliefs or their actions.

Finally, we come to the third quality that will help us survive: **Grace**. *Think Remarkable* lays out a framework for cultivating grace. In the world today there is so much divisiveness, discrimination, and conflict. Thus, the importance of graciousness—of understanding, empathy, and communal solidarity—cannot be overstated.

Nature's ecosystems thrive on symbiotic relationships and so must we. Human societies and businesses must cultivate collaborative relationships and work together to solve the multitudes of problems that seem to always be getting worse. So, argues Guy, we must foster relationships that are not only transactional but transformational.

Think Remarkable is not just a typical self-help narrative: it challenges us not only to improve our own individual lives but also to create a positive impact on the world around us. It makes a compelling case that each of us, equipped with growth, grit, and grace, can become catalysts for change.

The ideas presented within these pages are not merely aspirational; they suggest actionable steps that we can take to move us toward a more equitable and harmonious world.

As we confront the myriad challenges of our era—from social inequality to climate change, from loss of biodiversity to conflict and war—the suggestions laid out in *Think Remarkable* remind us of our shared responsibility to think, act, and live with purpose.

In these troubling, uncertain—and for some of us, desperate— times, it is imperative that we strive to work together. In other words, we must all live remarkably to make this a better, fairer, and happier world. And this book is a call for immediate action: the future of life on earth, including our own, depends on how we act now.

Jane Goodalll, PhD, DBE
Founder of the Jane Goodall Institute and
UN Messenger of Peace

Introduction

What a wonderful thought it is that some of the best days of our lives haven't happened yet.

—Anne Frank

Think Different

In 1997 I was Apple's chief evangelist, and I was in the room when Lee Clow of Apple's advertising agency, Chiat\Day, presented the Think Different campaign to Steve Jobs.

There were perhaps ten marketing people in the meeting, and Lee's presentation took our breath away because it so perfectly captured the spirit of Macintosh and Apple.

Here's to the crazy ones, the misfits, the rebels, the troublemakers, the round pegs in the square holes . . . the ones who see things differently—they're not fond of rules . . . . You can quote them, disagree with them, glorify or vilify them, but the only thing you can't do is ignore them because they change things . . . they push the human race forward, and while some may see them as the crazy ones, we see genius, because the ones who are crazy enough to think that they can change the world, are the ones who do.

—*Ad copy of Think Different*

Figure I.1   Poster from Apple's Think Different campaign which featured photos of Pablo Picasso, Albert Einstein, Martha Graham, Nelson Mandela, Amelia Earhart, and other remarkable people, 1997.

(Source: Nate Kawasaki)

Back then, Apple wasn't doing well. In fact, most of the pundits predicted that Apple would soon go bankrupt. Michael Dell (yes, that "Dell") even suggested that Apple return its cash to shareholders and close up shop. Sticking with Apple in those days was an act of faith and thinking differently.

To massively state the obvious, Michael Dell and the pundits were wrong. The Think Different campaign and the iMac line of Macintoshes rekindled the flame and saved Apple. The turnaround that Steve engineered was remarkable, and Apple became the most valuable company in history.

It's been a few decades since that meeting. The world has come a long way, but many problems still exist, new challenges have arisen, and much work remains to be done. However, there are also great opportunities. Now it's necessary to go beyond "think different" and go all the way to "think remarkable" to transform your life and the world.

The Big Picture

Suppose someone who is twice your age and holds a powerful political office tries to humiliate you. His reason was that you took offense to his insight on who needs abortions. Let's start with the words Congressman Matt Gaetz spoke in July 2022 at the Turning Point USA Student Action Summit:

> *Why is it that the women with the least likelihood of getting pregnant are the ones most worried about having abortions? Nobody wants to impregnate you if you look like a thumb.*

He offended many people with his statement. Among them was Olivia Julianna. She is a "queer, plus size, Latina activist" in her twenties, and she fired off a tweet in response:

> *It's come to my attention that Matt Gaetz—alleged pedophile—has said that it's always the "odious . . . 5'2 350 pound" women that "nobody wants to impregnate" who rally for abortion. I'm actually 5'11. 6'4 in heels. I wear them so the small men like you are reminded of your place.*

Gaetz returned fire with of photo of Julianna with a tweet that said, "Dander raised." Olivia then turned the controversy into a fundraising effort for abortion rights that raised $2.5 million.

She is a beacon to Gen Z and is leading the transition of power to the next generation alongside others such as Malala Yousafzai, David Hogg, Greta Thunberg, and Maxwell Frost.

The goal of this book is to help you make a difference, just like Julianna. First, let's define what being remarkable means. It does not mean amassing wealth, power, or fame. There are people who have done this and are not remarkable. And there are people who haven't and are.

In my book, being remarkable means you are making a difference and making the world a better place. However, you are not competing with Olivia, Jane Goodall, or Steve Jobs—although I won't dissuade you if that's your goal. Just know that it's enough to improve one life (even your own), one organization, one habitat, or one classroom.

Being remarkable also means you are a good person—people use words such as empathetic, honest, and compassionate to describe you. If offered the chance, they would love to join your *ohana*, the Hawaiian word for the community of people who support and care for you.

I can provide the roadmap, along with some inspirational examples, but only you can do the work. Being remarkable is neither innate nor conferred—if it were, you wouldn't need this book.

Sources

I used two sources of information and inspiration to write this book. The first source is several hundred remarkable people. Although they were not necessarily wealthy, powerful, or famous, they all made the world a better place. They personify empathy, resilience, creativity, and grace.

They were guests on my podcast, *Remarkable People*, and include people such as Olivia, Jane Goodall, Stacey Abrams, Mark Rober, Carol Dweck, Ken Robinson, Steve Wozniak, Margaret Atwood, Julia Cameron, Temple Grandin, and Bob Cialdini, to name a few.

The second source is my firsthand experiences. I've been the chief evangelist of Apple and Canva, worked for Google and Mercedes-Benz, and started three companies. All told, I've been a son, father, husband, "uncle," brother, evangelist, entrepreneur, investor, author, speaker, podcaster, mentor, ATM, and Wikipedia trustee.

Structure

> Twenty-volume folios will never make a revolution. It's the little pocket pamphlets that are to be feared.
>
> —Voltaire

Nonfiction books tend to be a vast morass of 300-page tomes that extol one idea. I should know—I've written several of them. In this book, however, less is more, so it is as succinct as possible. There are three *parts*:

• Growth	Build Your Foundation
• Grit	Implement Your Aspirations
• Grace	Uplift and Inspire

Growth, grit, and grace are necessary to make a difference. I present them in approximate sequential order, but becoming remarkable isn't necessarily linear. Feel free to jump around the book as your needs dictate.

Each part of this book consists of three *chapters*. Each chapter, in turn, contains *sections* that explain methods for achieving the chapter's objective. Each section begins with an assessment of who can use the section's ideas.

I mention dozens of individuals in this book. It's unlikely that you will recognize everyone. To help you identify them, there is a "List of Profiles" at the end of this book.

In summary, utilizing a few real-world examples, circa 2023, *Think Remarkable* is:

- *The Elements of Style,* not *The Chicago Manual of Style*
- Tinder, not eHarmony
- TikTok, not TED

Let's Do This!

Making a difference and being remarkable are not easy, but you won't regret trying. When you make a difference and are remarkable, you live a life that matters, reflects your best self, and inspires others to be remarkable as well.

One last subtle but critical point. The remarkable people I interviewed did not decide one day to be remarkable and then dedicate their life to this goal. Their motivation was outward focused and tactical: save a species, rise from poverty, invent a cool device, save democracy, and the like.

In pursuing these kinds of goals, they became remarkable, but "becoming remarkable" wasn't their objective. This book isn't about how to "repackage," "rebrand," or "reposition" yourself.

My message is simple: If you do remarkable things and make a difference, people will call you remarkable. In fact, you couldn't stop them if you tried. So let's get started.

Guy Kawasaki
Santa Cruz, California 2023

There's one more story inside the story of Lee Clow showing us the Think Different campaign. At the end of the meeting, he said to Steve, "I have two copies of these ads. I'll give one to you and one to Guy."

Steve, as only Steve would, responded, "Don't give Guy a copy. Just give me a copy."

For me, this was a man-or-mouse moment that you don't want to look back on and think, "Why did I wimp out?"

So I didn't. Right then and there, in front of everyone, I came back with, "Don't you trust me, Steve?"

And he came back with, "I don't."

And I came back with, "That's okay, Steve, because I don't trust you either."

That probably cost me a few million dollars in stock options, but it was worth it.

STAGE

1

Growth—Build a Foundation

1 | Adopt the Growth Mindset

Replace "Why is this happening to me?" with "What is this trying to teach me?"

—Nate Kawasaki

Embrace the Growth Mindset

∠ You want to overcome being told you can't accomplish something.
∠ You want to stop telling *yourself* you can't accomplish something.
∠ You're tired of worrying about jeopardizing your reputation and self-image.

I am not a remarkable hockey player or surfer. I took up these sports at the ages of forty-four and sixty, respectively. This means that I started thirty-four and fifty years too late, respectively.

My sons wanted to play hockey after we attended a San Jose Sharks game, so I started playing hockey even though I was old and from Hawaii. The closest thing to pond hockey where I grew up is shave ice. (Several people have pointed out that the correct term is "shaved ice." I grew up in Hawaii and have eaten more shave ice than all of them put together. The correct term is "shave ice," brah.)

In 2015, I started surfing because of my daughter. She was fourteen, and I was sixty. Despite growing up in Hawaii, I didn't have enough of a growth mindset to try something outside of studying and organized team sports, so surfing was new to me.

I embraced these new sports because Brenda Ueland and Carol Dweck profoundly impacted my mindset. Ueland was a teacher of writing at the University of Minnesota and authored a book called *If You Want to Write*.

My wife gave me Ueland's book in 1989 because I thought I wanted to write a book. However, my mindset at the time was that I was not a "writer" because I didn't have a degree in English, nor any formal training for the task. Ueland's book made me realize that maybe I could write a book because it contained these lessons:

- Don't worry about special training or anyone's permission and blessing to write. Just write.
- Write from the heart about what you know and love—not about what you think people expect from "writers." Just write.
- Shove aside judgments and criticisms of your writing—from both you and from others. Just write.

In short, I wrote my first book, *The Macintosh Way*, because of Ueland's book. Now fast-forward to 2006. Carol Dweck, a professor of psychology at Stanford University, releases her book *Mindset: The New Psychology of Success*. Her insights were like Ueland's but on steroids.

Her book convinced me that growth can happen along any path that you let it. At the time, I was fat, dumb, and happy concentrating on what worked for me in the past. I certainly wasn't taking up any new sports.

Dweck didn't just dent my universe; she expanded it. I had written a few books, but I was afraid of failure and embarrassment in other fields. Here is how Carol explains the fixed and growth mindsets:

The fixed mindset is the belief that your qualities are carved in stone. But your qualities can be cultivated through effort, good strategies, and lots of help, support, and mentorship from others.

People with a fixed mindset make statements such as "I'm too old to learn a new skill," or "I'm good at programming, but I could never learn marketing." People with a growth mindset, by contrast, are willing, if not eager, to explore and experiment.

Undoubtedly, the growth mindset is necessary to be remarkable, and you hold the power to change and elevate yourself. Full stop. Not negotiable. Let this sink in: if you want to be remarkable, you have to grow.

Learning hockey and surfing were difficult at my advanced age, but embracing these sports provided some of the most satisfying moments of my life. My moderate success in both sports showed me the benefits of a growth mindset and, more importantly, set my expectations to be able to learn new skills in general.

Find Support

- ∠ You want to learn how to identify people who can help you embrace the growth mindset.
- ∠ You're wondering how to assess whether an organization supports and implements the growth mindset.
- ∠ You want to search for a career with promising potential, yet be free of the traditional "nine to five" career.

If adopting the growth mindset was a personal decision and transition, life would be simple. However, growing requires both supportive people and a supportive environment. According to Carol:

It's not just growth mindset people, it's growth mindset environments that allow you to use that mindset effectively.

It's not like you have your growth mindset and you take it with you, and you are challenge seeking and resilient. The environment you're in matters.

The way to find people who foster the growth mindset is to look at their track records. Struggle and change are good things because they mean the people had to grow:

- Have they overcome hardship and setbacks, or have they lived on Easy Street their whole lives?
- Did they major in one academic area and end up working in a seemingly unrelated role or industry?
- Once in the workforce, did they change industries and functions?
- Do they interact with a diverse selection of people? Their social media accounts are probably a window into their soul.
- Are they busy? Jane Goodall, who lives in the United Kingdom, spoke in Denver, Chicago, Madison, and Tampa Bay in March 2023. There's a reason busy people are busy.

However, you may be working inside existing organizations for most of your career, so the ability to find individuals with the growth mindset isn't enough. You also need to find *environments* that support a growth mindset.

Here are ways to do this:

- Study the organization's "public face" in the form of press releases, blog posts, social media, and speeches by executives as well as reviews on sites where people rate places to work.
- Understand that few large, established organizations have a growth mindset (or for that matter a fixed mindset) from top to bottom. You want to work on a team *within* the organization that supports growth, so look for pockets of growth.
- Ask the people who work there what their team is like, as well as the organization in general. People with growth mindsets usually work in teams with growth mindsets too.
- Look for formal learning, development, diversity, and social-responsibility programs. While they might be "window dressing," at least it shows the organization is trying.

My recommendation is to avoid organizations where a fixed mindset is already institutionalized. The people there may have good intentions—perhaps to avoid failure from risky actions—but that also stifles innovation and change.

Focus instead on finding organizations and individuals with a growth mindset who can foster your own growth mindset. Go to the light—and then become the light for others.

Embrace Change

∠ You're wondering if you should do just a few things well or go where you have not gone before.

∠ You want to use what you've learned in your career and apply it to other issues.

∠ You want to learn to break away from stereotypical constraints to expand your knowledge and skill set.

Your mindset can only grow to the extent that you expose it to new experiences, domains of knowledge, and skill sets. You can accomplish this in several ways:

- Study subjects that you've never considered—or that you failed at in the past.
- Explore areas you've kept putting off because you didn't think you'd excel at them.
- Adopt the interests of your family, friends, and followers instead of making them embrace yours.
- Experiment with new tools and technologies and see where they take you.

My earlier stories of embracing hockey and surfing pale in comparison to the growth of two NASA rocket scientists: Mark Rober and Wanda Harding. Here are their stories.

Mark began his career at NASA, where he worked on the design of the Curiosity rover that went to Mars. On the side, he tinkered with a Halloween costume that used two iPads to simulate seeing through his clothes and flesh. A YouTube video of this costume went viral.

After NASA, he took a job at Apple working on virtual reality in cars to prevent motion sickness. He continued making videos that attracted millions of followers and the scrutiny of Apple management. Ask any Gen Zer about his videos showing thieves getting sprayed with glitter and fart gas when they opened stolen packages as well as his "Squirrelympics."

He continues to create YouTube videos to interest people in physics, math, and science. He's added a line of scientific toys under the CrunchLabs label. He hopes to be a high school physics teacher someday. His mindset has grown from engineer to evangelist to educator, while always being a prankster.

At the end of our interview, he told me this:

I want to teach in a class. This is what I love about teachers: they're the ultimate investors in human capital. I am the product of some amazing teachers who are then themselves products of teachers before them.

With the teachers, you don't really ever get to see the full impact of your work. But you are investing in people who will then go off and hopefully do amazing things and inspire other folks.

There must be growth-mindset chemicals in the water at NASA because Wanda Harding worked there too. She started her career as a project manager for an electrical contractor. This means she was managing the crew wiring renovated buildings in Georgia.

She was the senior mission manager at NASA and oversaw the mission that sent the Curiosity rover to Mars. Then she became a technical director at NOAA and oversaw polar orbiting environmental monitoring satellite ground systems.

She has progressed from stars to students because after these careers, she returned to Piedmont College in order to prepare for teaching science to high-need students in Georgia. She shifted from telescope to microscope when she answered a calling to teach science, mathematics, and physics to high school students.

To grow your mindset, embrace change by pursuing new areas outside your comfort zone like my two NASA alumni friends. Mark and Wanda expanded their mindsets from rocket science into making

Figure 1.1   Mark Rober with a NERF gun ten times the size of a normal one, 2016. He was on a quest to make the world's largest and smallest NERF guns. The "bullets" were made out of toilet plungers.

(Source: Madisun Nuismer)

science videos and teaching high school students, showing how remarkable people can grow and make a difference.

Go Farther

∠ You're wondering if you should stick with interests that do not entail money and connections.

∠ You're looking for inspirational examples of making a difference through spirited and long-term commitment.

∠ You find yourself thinking of only the future instead of the importance of your present endeavors.

There are multiple paths for people with a growth mindset. First, you can stick to one path and go further along it than anyone (including yourself and your parents) would have predicted.

Remarkable people often recount their childhood experiences in order to explain where they ended up. For example, here is Jane Goodall reminiscing about her youth in the 1930s:

> *I used to roam on the cliffs with my dog, and that's where I watched the birds and the squirrels and read Dr. Doolittle. I wished I could have a parrot to teach me animal language. And when I was eight, I pretended to all my friends that I could understand animals. I interpreted the dogs barking and the cats meowing and the birds singing.*

In 1941, at the age of seven, she read *The Story of Doctor Dolittle*, and that's when she decided she must go to Africa one day. Through the rest of her childhood she showed a love for animals and a fascination for how they lived.

Her family could not afford to send her to college, so she went to secretarial school to learn how to type, take shorthand, and do book-keeping. Jane ended up in Nairobi, where she met Louis Leakey and

Figure 1.2   Jane Goodall with Figan, the alpha male, at Gombe National Park in Tanzania.

(Source: Jane Goodall Institute)

wound up working as Leakey's secretary. Leakey was the British anthropologist who documented the origin of human beings in East Africa.

In 1957 Leakey told Jane about some chimpanzees living near a lake in Tanganyika. Jane's research on chimpanzees began in 1960 when she was in her mid-twenties and continued for sixty years. She proved that chimpanzees were not simply wild animals but were intelligent and highly social.

By 2023 Goodall had received honorary doctorates from over seventy universities. She is a member of the National Academy of Sciences and the Royal Society of London. She was named one of *Time* magazine's 100 most influential people in the world in 2018, and she won the Templeton Prize in 2021.

Jane's career demonstrates that one path to remarkableness is to persevere in a field and achieve greater success than expected. It may take a long time, but those who persevere are often rewarded.

Change Horses

∠ You want to learn the benefits of pivoting to an entirely different field or interest.
∠ You want confirmation that the destination, not the starting point, is what matters most.
∠ You're wondering if it's ever too late to change your plans.

A second path for people with a growth mindset is to "change horses" and pursue an entirely different field. Admittedly, my knowledge of horses is limited to watching five seasons of Paramount Network's *Yellowstone* series, but consider the path of Julia Child, author and television star of French cuisine.

She was born to a wealthy family in Pasadena, California, and graduated from Smith College in Massachusetts where she majored in history. She began her career in New York as a copywriter for W. & J. Sloane, a furniture store.

In World War II, she was too tall to join the Women's Army Corp, so she went to work for the Office of Strategic Services (OSS), the

Figure 1.3   Julia Child in her Cambridge, Massachusetts, kitchen, 1974.

(Source: Science History Images/Alamy Stock Photo)

predecessor of the CIA. In other words, Julia was a spy. She started as a typist (like Jane Goodall) but quickly rose in the organization.

One of her projects was to develop a repellant to ward off sharks from exploding underwater mines meant for German submarines. She was later posted to Sri Lanka and China. She married Paul Cushing Child in 1946, and he introduced her to French cuisine when she was approximately thirty-four years old.

Five years later she graduated from Le Cordon Bleu cooking school in France. She began teaching French cooking to Americans in Paris and developing recipes that eventually became the bestseller that she co-authored with Louisette Bertholle and Simone Beck called *Mastering the Art of French Cooking*.

Her writing and appearances led to the television show called *The French Chef*. It ran for ten years and won a Peabody and an Emmy. The books and television shows she created until her death in 2004 are too numerous to mention. All this from a woman who didn't learn to cook in her youth because her wealthy family had a cook.

Going further along a path than anticipated or veering off onto a new path are both viable options. The destination, not the starting point, is what matters, regardless of the path's linearity.

Take Baby Steps

∠ You want to learn if it's small steps or huge transformations that lead to long-term success.

∠ You're wondering if what you're doing now will pay off in the long run.

∠ You're searching for ways to catch up to your peers that appear to have zoomed ahead of you.

Until you've got the growth mindset flowing through your neurons, set small goals so that success begets success. You don't need to star in a Hollywood film, become an investigative reporter for the *New York Times*, start a billion-dollar company, or teach at Harvard as a first step.

Growth isn't going to occur in leaps and bounds or moments of miraculous epiphanies. It's much more likely to happen in baby steps. Let's say that you want to become a writer. Start with a personal journal, write for *Medium*, submit opinion pieces and letters to the editor, and keep going from there.

The first place my writing was published was the Apple developer's newsletter in the mid-1980s. My seminal article for this prestigious publication, circulation 1,000, was called "The Silicon Valley Guide to Dating." Because I was in charge of software evangelism, I was the publisher and editor of the newsletter, which ensured the article's publication.

My first book was *The Macintosh Way*, published in 1987. It explained the philosophies and tactics of the Macintosh Division of Apple. Scott, Foresman published the book because I was a highly visible Apple executive at the time. When I look at it now, the writing quality embarrasses me.

But I've been writing ever since.

There's nothing wrong with baby steps. In fact, that's how the world works. You are deluding yourself if you think that you will have a choice between instant success and a long grind. The long grind is what prepares you for ultimate, long-lasting success.

Embrace Envy

∠ You're inspired by remarkable young people such as Olivia Julianna, Malala Yousafzai, and Maxwell Frost and you're wondering if your motivation is as noble as theirs.

∠ You're wondering if you can ever make a big difference in the world.

∠ You want to learn how to turn envy into a legitimate source of inspiration and purpose.

From the outside looking in, or the present looking back, you may attribute the motivation of remarkable people to making a difference, saving the planet, or to creating astounding works of art, music, and writing.

More power to you if this is true for you, but you are not alone if less lofty goals are your motivation. This is how Steve Wozniak explained the formation of Apple to me:

> His [Steve Jobs's] idea was not a computer company. His idea was what he knew. He'd sold surplus electronic parts. He knew how to buy switches and capacitors and transistors and sell them, and even some little low-level chips.. . .
>
> He wanted to start out and just make a PC board that would cost us twenty bucks a board to build, and we'd sell them for forty bucks. Neither one of us could really come up with a good argument that we'd make money, but he said, "Well, at least for once in our life, we'd have a company."
>
> One thing he wanted was to somehow be important in the world, and he didn't have the academic background or really the business background, but he had at least me, and so he said, "Let's start a company."

I can relate to this kind of thinking. When I was a teenager, someone gave me a ride in his Porsche 911. In college, a classmate's father

Figure 1.4 You've got to love Woz. Here he is playing Segway polo in Cologne, Germany, 2023.

(Source: Action Press via ZUMA Press)

drove his Ferrari 275 GT to the Stanford Family Weekend and gave me a ride in it. Then Mike Boich's mother let me drive her Ferrari Daytona. (Mike Boich was my college classmate and the guy who gave me a job at Apple.)

These were mind-expanding experiences for a boy from a poor part of Honolulu. Envy drove both of us. Steve envied people who were important. I envied people who drove nice cars. I didn't care about changing the world; I just wanted to change the car, and this is what motivated me to study hard and work hard.

There's another kind of envy that works too. This happens when you are in the presence of greatness, and you want to be like that person. For example, you might envy a performing artist, a writer, or an athlete for their ability and for their impact on the people around them.

Embracing these feelings of envy can be motivating and thus productive. The most important thing is that you are motivated, so don't stress about your motivation's source.

Find a Hero

∠ You want to learn how to deal with issues that directly hinder what you want to do.

∠ You seek inspiration from people who overcame such a situation.

∠ You want to gain perspective to stay motivated and to avoid self-pity.

After more than twenty years of dealing with tinnitus, vertigo, and hearing loss, by early 2022 I was almost completely deaf. I attribute this to years of listening to crappy pitches from tech entrepreneurs.

Until my cochlear implant was activated in September of that year, I depended on live transcription to conduct podcast interviews. Live transcription wasn't great back then, so it was a struggle to be my usual conversational self.

During this period, I needed a hero to get past this handicap, and one thought occurred to me and kept me going. If Beethoven could compose music while deaf, then I could record podcasts by reading live transcriptions while deaf (not that I'm anywhere near Beethoven in talent).

Still, podcasting while deaf is still easier than applying for a doctorate while in prison. Stanley Andrisse is an endocrinologist and assistant professor at the Howard University College of Medicine and the author of *From Prison Cells to PhD: It Is Never Too Late to Do Good*.

His remarkable journey started in Ferguson-Florissant, Missouri, and includes three felony convictions. He was incarcerated when he began his pursuit of a doctorate, and he encountered prison regulations that banned any letter over five pages.

Unfortunately, information packets and applications from schools are far longer than five pages. So he had the material sent to a friend, who then broke it down into five-page letters and mailed them separately.

Thus, each school involved ten to twenty letters, and he applied to seven programs. Mail doesn't necessarily arrive together, so he had to reassemble the pieces upon receipt. Another problem was the limit on the amount of mail that prisoners can have in their cell, so guards confiscated what was coming to him.

Filling out online forms was difficult too. Each application required a research statement and a personal statement. Stanley sent his handwritten draft to a friend for editing. These were sent back to Stanley for changes, and then Stanley sent the corrected copies to his girlfriend for typing. She in turn sent the completed essays to other friends who were copying his responses into online forms and submitting them on his behalf.

All told, six people were helping him apply to seven doctorate programs. The process took months. One question on the applications was a showstopper: "Have you ever been convicted of a felony? If yes, please explain." There was space for only a two-line answer on each application.

Six of the seven schools rejected his application, but Saint Louis University gave him a second chance, and Stanley was able to go from prison to PhD.

It helps to have a hero to put your "plight" into perspective and reduce tendencies to focus on the negative. Struggles are valid and worthy of attention, but perseverance is one of the things that makes people remarkable.

Bloom, Baby, Bloom

Raquel Willis is an activist and author. She was the executive editor of *Out* magazine and national organizer for the Transgender Law Center. Of all the people I've interviewed, her transition is one of the most dramatic: from a "little black boy" to a position of prominence and leadership in the LGBTQ+ community. The journey involved hormonal replacement therapy and "bottom surgery," as well as major psychological adjustments.

Figure 1.5   Raquel Willis at New York Fashion Week, 2019.

(Source: Jamie McCarthy/Getty Images)

Her memoir is called *The Risk It Takes to Bloom: On Life and Liberation*. Here's how she explained what her growth and transition took in our interview:

After being raised as a little black boy in the American South to the woman that I am today, an activist, and an author . . . on the surface that transition seems very drastic, but honestly, I think we all have transitions throughout our life.

The keys to my transition have been trusting my inner voice . . . the conviction about who I am, even when the world doesn't understand, or even when it feels like there's this mountain of work that I'm going to have to do to get the world to understand.

It's also been about not allowing those lows in life or those tragedies that we all inevitably face to be so thoroughly destabilizing that they keep me from seeing a capacity for change, a capacity for growth.

> *The biggest key to not just surviving but thriving is just having humility and understanding that I'm just one within a larger collective and that my singular life story is just a thread within this larger, rich tapestry of a bunch of other stories.*

Growth and transition are challenging and time-consuming, but they are essential to making a difference and being remarkable. They demand conviction, humility, and considerable effort to achieve.

Additional Resources

- Andrisse, Stanley. *From Prison Cells to PhD: It Is Never Too Late to Do Good.*
- Child, Julia. *My Life in France.*
- Dweck, Carol. *Mindset: The New Psychology of Success.*
- Willis, Raquel. *The Risk It Takes to Bloom: On Life and Liberation.*

2 | Embrace Vulnerability

Growth and comfort never coexist.

—Ginni Rometty

Flip Over Growth

∠ You want to learn if successful people were vulnerable when they started.

∠ You want inspiration from those who overcame failure.

∠ You aim to transform setbacks into growth.

The flip side of the growth mindset is vulnerability. The word comes from the Latin noun *vulnus,* which means "wound." Becoming remarkable will take a long time, and you will face failure and setback, so the journey entails embracing vulnerability. And that's if things go well.

Everyone is vulnerable. Everyone encounters wounds to their self-image, reputation, and well-being. Everyone. More important than avoiding wounds is how you deal with them. I recommend approaching failure this way: sometimes you win and sometimes you grow.

If the fear of wounds prevents you from taking chances, then you are stuck. You may be stuck in a low place or a high place, but in either case you won't achieve your full potential.

Not giving up after a setback separates remarkable people from mundane people. Few people know that Kristi Yamaguchi finished twelfth in her first figure skating competition, but that only motivated her to increase her efforts. She went on to win the 1992 Olympic figure skating championship, as well as two world championships and the sixth season of *Dancing with the Stars*.

Figure 2.1　Kristi Yamaguchi waves to the crowd after winning the gold medal at the 1992 Winter Olympics. She came a long way from finishing 12th in her first competition.

(Source: David Madison / Getty Images)

The key is to learn to embrace vulnerability, which entails accepting that setbacks may occur and continuing regardless. Ironically, this will make you stronger and better able to overcome "wounds" over time.

"Go on, Be Brave"

∠ You want to learn how people have overcome challenges and limitations to achieve extraordinary goals.

∠ You want to put the challenges that you face into perspective.

∠ You want to understand the power of resilience, determination, and adaptability.

In 2014, Andrea Lytle Peet was diagnosed with ALS, a degenerative nerve disease that destroys cells in the brain and spinal cord. Most people succumb to ALS within two to five years as they lose their ability to eat, breathe, walk, and talk.

Figure 2.2   Andrea Lytle Peet finishing her fiftieth marathon after she was diagnosed with ALS. This one was the Prince of Wales Island Marathon in Alaska, 2022.

(Source: Shannon Murphy)

As of 2023 Andrea has survived for nine years, and after her initial diagnosis, she had a brave idea: complete a marathon in all fifty states in defiance of the disease and to garner support to find its cure. To do this, she had to be brave and make herself vulnerable to physical danger as well as to disappointment.

She started her quest running on two legs but ended it in a recumbent trike. She achieved her goal in May 2022 in Prince of Wales Island, Alaska. However, finishing in Alaska wasn't the original plan. She wanted her fiftieth race to be the Boston Marathon (more on that in a minute).

Striving to complete fifty marathons after a diagnosis of a fatal nerve disease is the embodiment of embracing vulnerability. She decided to "go on and be brave," which is the name of the movie about her race against time.

Brace for Impact

∠ You want to view difficulties and obstacles as a doorway to growth.
∠ You want to learn how to anticipate potential problems and plan for setbacks.
∠ You're wondering how maintaining perspective can help you handle life's difficulties.

To be blunt, shit is going to happen. You will face negativity, rejection, and even danger. People will tell you that what you want to do can't be done, shouldn't be done, and isn't necessary.

Every remarkable person I know has dealt with challenges. This is what Andrea Lytle Peet went through after learning of her ALS diagnosis:

> I remember just after my diagnosis I was sitting in the car crying. I was so depressed, and I looked up and I just realized that I can be depressed, or I can live my life now. Time will pass the same way either way.

But wait, if you thought a diagnosis of ALS was bad, there's more. The Boston Athletic Association rejected her application to the

Boston Marathon. There are divisions for wheelchair users, para-athletes, handcycle, duo teams, and individuals who are visually, physi-cally, and mentally impaired, but somehow Andrea and her leg-powered recumbent trike were ineligible.

You would think the Marathon folks would be ecstatic about Andrea's brave quest, but nope. The association's letter said this:

> *While we understand your position as outlined in your email, we are unable to allow participation by way of a recumbent trike as that falls within a cycling realm. Boston Marathon Para Athletics Division & Adaptive Program rules state that: "No handcycles with motors or pedals are permitted. No other gear, crank, or chain powered cycling equipment is permitted for use by athletes in the Boston Marathon including foot-powered recumbent bikes, tricycles, or bicycles."*

Here's a paragraph from Andrea's "in-your-face" response to the Boston Athletic Association:

> *Being diagnosed with ALS is like being told NO for your entire future. NO cure, NO treatment, NO chance of recovery, NO chance to have a baby, NO hope. But what I have learned is that there is always hope. You might just have to find a different way.*

So what did Andrea do? First, she checked off the state of Massa-chusetts by completing the more flexible and accommodating Mar-tha's Vineyard Marathon.

Team Drea, which consisted of her husband and a small group of friends, then traveled to Boston, where she "finished" the Boston Marathon course the day before the race. Ironically, this race marked the fifty-year anniversary of the women's division.

So after bravery, the next step is to brace for impact because it's coming.

- Accept that shit can happen, and probably will. Don't be shocked when things don't go well the first time or all the time.
- Identify the possibilities. Make a list of all the things that can go wrong and eliminate what you can in advance.

- Develop contingency plans to fix what you cannot prevent. It's better to do this in advance than in real time as the crisis is happening. But in any case, figure out a way, like doing a marathon before the official race.
- Maintain perspective. Ask yourself if what happened to you is so bad. For example, would you rather lose your hearing or be diagnosed with ALS?

There is no doubt that the world will occasionally shit on you. Remember that the discomfort is temporary; do what you can in the present, and keep in mind that with difficulty comes opportunities for growth—which is exactly what a remarkable person invites with open arms.

Give Yourself a Break

∠ You want to learn how to deal with the aftermath of vulnerability through your personal thoughts and actions.

∠ You want to face the negative effects head on and form actionable steps.

∠ You want to learn how to garner support from individuals who have also encountered falling short, yet overcame it.

After the impact and vulnerability occurs, you have to deal with the negative effects. This may entail financial loss, embarrassment, and blows to your self-confidence.

The first step in the process of bouncing back is to "give yourself a break" by forgiving yourself and stopping the self-criticism. Here are ways to give yourself a break:

- Acknowledge your disappointment. Don't go into denial.
- Find the silver lining. There's always something to learn from failure, which we discuss in the next section.
- Obtain the support of others. Contrary to the old saying, misery hates company, so don't isolate yourself.

- Set new goals. The way to get past a failure is to succeed the next time.
- Take action. Goals don't achieve themselves, so get back in action and work at them.

It's important to know that everyone has come up short—even Steve Jobs, Jane Goodall, and Stacey Abrams. Especially Guy Kawasaki. When you come up short, it means you're pushing yourself, which is a good thing. If you never fall short, you are not pushing yourself, which is not how to become remarkable.

Learn from Failure

∠ You want to understand how failure is perceived by others.
∠ You're looking for inspirational examples of remarkable people who experienced failure.
∠ You want to figure out how to determine if an opportunity could be a likely failure.

When you start to embrace vulnerability, consider what's truly at risk. For many people, the risk is embarrassment, so maybe they'd take more risks if they could fail anonymously. But trying to hide your failures isn't worth the effort.

To begin with, few people will probably notice you flop, fizzle, or misfire. And those who do notice won't care or remember it. When I started surfing, I thought everyone laughed when they saw me falling. After a while, I realized that few saw and even fewer cared. I could even fall on increasingly bigger waves in even more spectacular ways without ramification.

Consider Apple: the most valuable company of all time failed with the Apple III, Lisa, Newton, Pippin, and iPod Hi-Fi. You may have never heard of these Apple products, and I won't waste space explaining what they were.

Failing in a careless, unconcerned, or offhand manner is not okay. Failure is a waste of money, time, effort, and human potential. It can

Figure 2.3   Apple's Lisa computer was released in 1983.
It was a commercial failure but paved the way for Macintosh.
(Source: Apple)

harm the careers of employees, and in extreme cases it can endanger
the lives of customers, employees, and vendors.

Failures provide valuable information that improve future efforts.
They are not simply a waste of time and resources. And you could not
have obtained this information in any other way than risking failure.

Here are three examples from the field of entertainment:

- Walt Disney was fired from one of his first animation jobs
  because the editor felt he lacked imagination.
- Oprah Winfrey was fired from her first job in television as a
  news anchor in Baltimore.
- Steven Spielberg was rejected by the USC film school multiple times.

The point is that failure is less destructive and sometimes even
constructive if it can be transformed into something that ultimately
strengthens you. The path to remarkableness is not paved.

Use the Doubters

∠ You want to use people's doubts to motivate you to prove them wrong.

∠ You're wondering if there is a positive aspect to negative and destructive feedback.

∠ You want to learn the importance of your "village."

Growing up was hell for Jonathan Conyers. He was the youngest of five kids, and both his parents were crack addicts. By the time he graduated from high school, he had been forced to move more than ten times from homeless shelters and low-income housing. The money his parents made went to buy crack, so his family had to steal food and clothes.

After an arrest for burglary, he entered the Frederick Douglass Academy in Harlem as a condition to avoid incarceration. In order to evade the danger and illicit actions of classmates in the school cafeteria, Jonathan started attending the debate team meetings, and it was there that he found his calling and his mentor, K.M. DiColandrea.

It would be easy to say, "And the rest is history," but this would not be accurate. Jonathan's high-school journey was filled with drugs, alcohol, guns, near-death and near-arrest experiences, and teenage pregnancy.

By pure grit and resilience, with a side helping of luck, Jonathan persevered. He graduated from the State University of New York at Stony Brook with a degree in respiratory therapy. His story was featured in the blog *Humans of New York*. To achieve this success, he had to build a village because he wasn't born into one.

In our interview, he pointed out that his village even includes people who wanted to harm and impair him. Jonathan told me that their destructive feedback was useful to him because it motivated him to prove them wrong:

> *I consider those people a part of my village because they helped build my confidence. They helped build my awareness. They put me in situations of adversity and situations of doubt.*

> *I showed that in those moments I was able to overcome, and I was able to step up to any challenge . . . there were a lot of moments just being born into the life I was born into, being born into the type of parents I had, being born into the ZIP codes I was born into.*
>
> *I couldn't read in the third grade and there was so many teachers who was willing to give up on me . . . who thought I should be a part of the system, who thought I should be another Black kid who will be a statistic.*

Has anyone told you that you can't succeed? They could be doing you a favor if you can turn their doubt and negativity into your determination. People like Jonathan have proven that you shouldn't let doubt go to waste.

Face It Until You Make It

∠ You want to learn how to overcome fear and attain your goals through strategic steps.

∠ You're wondering if faking confidence is a good strategy.

∠ You want to learn how to face bigger challenges with the confidence from previous accomplishments.

Later in the book, we will discuss the concept of "faking it until you make it" (acting confident when you are not). This chapter focuses on facing and dealing with vulnerabilities and "wounds."

Here are two examples. First, Sarah Frey is a pumpkin mogul. Her company controls 15,000 acres of farmland and sold eight million pumpkins in 2022, more than anyone else in the US.

When she was approximately nine years old, she and her father were driving a pickup truck in rural Illinois. They happened upon a garbage-can-sized snapping turtle weighing thirty-five or forty pounds. Her father told her to grab it and throw it in the back of the truck so they could eat it.

She eventually got the courage to do this. They're not called snapping turtles for nothing, and they are especially aggressive on land. In our interview, she credits this formative experience with helping her overcome later challenges, such as making sales calls on Walmart.

Second, few activities are riskier than big-wave surfing. Any surfing is dangerous, but imagine riding down the outside of a 100-foot-tall building moving at forty miles per hour. When such a wave crashes on you, this is what it feels like:

Imagine you're in a washing machine on spin cycle and then for lack of a better person, King Kong grabs the washing machine and starts shaking it in all directions.

This description is from Garrett McNamara. He should know because he's the big-wave surfer who made the world aware of the waves at Nazaré, Portugal. Depending on who you believe, he may have surfed the largest wave in history. The HBO series *100 Foot Wave* is based on his adventures around the world.

If there's a person in the world to ask how to push past fear and vulnerability, Garrett is it. This is how he explained the process to me:

When I was sixteen, I wouldn't go out over ten feet. I was terrified. I got pounded on a ten-foot wave, and I vowed to never surf a wave over ten feet.

Figure 2.4   Garrett McNamara at Nazaré, Portugal, surfing the mythical 100-foot wave, 2013. He's the dot at the end of the white foam.

(Source: Garrett McNamara)

And then my buddies forced me to go out. They gave me the right board, gave me the right advice, and I caught every wave I wanted, and that was it.

The fire was lit. I lived for big waves. I loved big waves from that day forward. It was ten feet and fifteen feet, then twenty feet, then twenty-five.

I got pounded on a solid fifty-foot face . . . the worst you could ever get pounded and came up laughing. So then I was like, "I can handle anything."

There isn't "faking it until you make it" in big-wave surfing. Death and dismemberment are the risks—not simply bruised feelings or crushed egos. Garrett is saying that you must confront your fears, and eventually they can turn to excitement. But be safe as you do this and remember that baby steps are okay!

Additional Resources

- Brown, Brené. *Daring Greatly: How the Courage to Be Vulnerable Transforms the Way We Live, Love, Parent, and Lead.*
- Peet, Andrea. *Hope Fights Back: Fifty Marathons and a Life-or-Death Race Against ALS.*

3 | Plant Many Seeds

The task of the modern educator is not to cut down jungles, but to irrigate deserts.

—C. S. Lewis

Get Stoked About Oaks

∠ You'd like to see if the metaphor of planting acorns is applicable to being remarkable.

∠ You're curious about how to plant oak trees.

∠ You're wondering if small starts can lead to big results.

There is a hill behind my house covered with eucalyptus trees. Many things that I love come from Australia, including Canva (online design), Cochlear (cochlear implant), Rode (podcast equipment), and Espresso (portable monitors), but eucalyptus trees are not one of them. Scientists estimate that eucalyptus trees use several hundred liters of water per day, and they are highly flammable because of their oil content. They also shed their bark, which adds to the supply of combustible material.

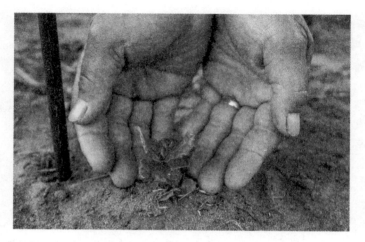

Figure 3.1   One of my six-month-old oak seedlings, September 2023. I will never be able to sit in its shade.

(Source: Beth Kawasaki)

You can't cut down some tree species in California, but it's open season on eucalyptus trees. I had 150 of this invasive species removed. (If you want eucalyptus chips or wood, let me know.) Then, faced with a denuded hill, my challenge was to repopulate it with a native species such as oaks.

These are beautiful trees that provide an ecosystem for caterpillars, birds, and other animals. Plus they also help water infiltrate the soil. Having become stoked about oaks, I learned that growing oaks is not a trivial task. In many ways, the process is a model for personal growth and preparation for a remarkable life.

For one thing, I had to face my mortality: I may never sit under the shade of any of these trees because of my age. The gist of the process for populating a hill with oaks is this:

- Gather hundreds of acorns from the ground beneath existing trees. Acorns are free, abundant, and barely noticed by most people. University Avenue in downtown Los Gatos, California, is a good place to look if you live in the San Francisco Bay Area.

- Identify the bad acorns by dropping them in water. If they float, they are rotten or dead. If they sink, they are healthy. (The analogy to life breaks down a little here.)
- Place them in a refrigerator under damp paper towels for a month or two. This is called stratification—it simulates the exposure to cold that acorns experience in the wild that prepares them for germination.
- Plant them an inch below the surface in the field. Water and feed them. Watch what happens and eliminate the weak ones. Most will not sprout. Forget "plug and play." This process is "plant and pray."
- Water and feed them, then wait for twenty years. Then behold what a magnificent tree can grow from a tiny seed.

The metaphor of planting acorns is perfect for making a difference and being remarkable. That is, you must collect, prepare, plant, tend, and wait. It is as simple to describe as it is difficult to accomplish.

Trust the Dots

∠ You want to know if the path to success is straightforward and predictable.

∠ You want to know if it's okay to follow your heart.

∠ You want to learn how to trust and tend to all endeavors equally.

Less than a year after I planted my acorns, I've already learned that it's impossible to predict which ones will sprout. This reminds me of a quote from Steve Jobs's Stanford commencement address in 2005:

> *You can't connect the dots looking forward. You can only connect them looking backward. So you have to trust that the dots will somehow connect in your future.*
>
> *You have to trust in something, your gut, destiny, life, karma, whatever, because believing that the dots will connect down the road will give you the confidence to follow your heart even when it leads you off the well-worn path and that will make all the difference.*

Figure 3.2   Steve Jobs giving commencement address at Stanford University on June 12, 2005.

If we knew which acorns would grow into mighty oaks and which dots would connect, then we would tend only to those. The futility of this wishful thinking is Steve's point. You have to plant many seeds and trust that things will work out later.

Let's say, for example, that you wanted to get Jane Goodall on your podcast. Here is how the dots worked for me:

- 1967: An elementary school teacher in a low-income part of Honolulu convinces my parents to put me into a college prep school.
- 1972: I matriculate to Stanford, where I become friends with Mike Boich.
- 1978: I begin work in the jewelry business and learn how to sell.
- 1983: Mike hires me into Apple as the second Macintosh software evangelist.
- 2018: Ronit Widman-Levy, executive producer of TEDx Palo Alto, invites me to interview Jane Goodall.
- 2020: Jane Goodall accepts my invitation to be on my podcast.

Figure 3.3   On stage at TEDx Palo Alto with Jane Goodall—one of the high points of my career.

(Source: Nataliya Arditi)

I did not know Ronit. She only knew "of me" because of my work at Apple. Thus, all the dots that led to a career at Apple led to getting Jane Goodall on my podcast. I hope that you don't think that any of this was planned.

In Silicon Valley, we throw ideas against the wall, see what sticks, paint a bull's-eye around the winners, and then declare victory. At most, we are making intelligent guesses and hoping for the best. The best practice is to plant many seeds because the more seeds you plant, the more oaks will grow.

Get an Education

∠ You want to know if formal education is necessary to succeed.

∠ You're wondering if the process of learning can provide critical skills beyond just facts.

∠ You want to learn how to get educated if formal schooling isn't accessible.

There are few better ways to plant seeds than to get a formal education—in any subject, really, because an education can beget so much goodness:

- Exposure. Education opens new worlds—ones that you may not have encountered without schooling. Many people on my podcast mentioned how early education opened their eyes to new subjects.
- Critical thinking. Schools don't teach you only facts. They also help you learn how to think, judge, and decide. You can always use technology to retrieve facts. Critical thinking is harder.
- Social skills. Schools force you to interact with teachers and other students. Making a difference is seldom a solo act.
- Technical and manual skills. I define education broadly—from computer programming to auto repair, carpentry, and cooking. Lots of knowledge is necessary to make the world go round.
- Relationships. Even if you don't start the next Apple, your classmates are likely to plant many seeds in your life. As mentioned, I got my job at Apple through a classmate.
- Credibility. Like it or not, people ascribe credibility to educational degrees. I'm not saying they are necessary or sufficient, but they can help.

When I interviewed Joe Foster, the founder of Reebok, I learned that he and his brother went to college to learn about the shoe business even though they were third-generation shoemakers. I'll let him explain the "off the books" benefits that he gained.

Obviously working at the family business, we knew how to make football boots, rugby boots, soccer boots, whatever.

But we became friends with a lot of people who knew the answers to a lot of questions. Where do we get this machine from? Where do we get this material from? How do we do this? What are different techniques?

Alas, a formal education is a privilege that not everyone can exercise. I wish this were not true, because of the benefits listed above. However, there are at least three additional ways to get an education:

First, there is reading. This can occur before, during, and after formal education. For example, Stephen Wolfram, the youngest recipient of a MacArthur Fellowship (aka, "genius award"), told me this:

> *I kind of started reading books about physics and so on, and I discovered this amazing fact that you could just go to a library and find all these books and started learning stuff.*

According to Elizabeth Gruner, English professor at the University of Virginia, reading is magic:

> *Reading is a form of alchemy because it changes us . . . . It can transport us to places that we haven't been before. It can give us experiences that we wouldn't have otherwise, and then those experiences become part of us.*

Second, there is online education in forms such as courses, classes, and videos. Anyone with access to the Internet can obtain an education with some effort. Like reading, online education can lack many social aspects, but it still beats ignorance.

Third, there are apprenticeships, internships, and training programs. Some individuals may not consider them formal education, but that is their semantic problem. If you are learning something, it's education.

Formal education is neither a prerequisite nor a capstone to learning. Regardless of how it is obtained, education increases the seeds in your life. Remarkable individuals obtain an education and then never stop learning.

Pursue "Interests," Not "Passions"

∠ You want to know if you have fallen behind because you haven't found your "passion" yet.

∠ You're wondering if a passion is "love at first sight" or a long-term courtship.

∠ You want to learn how to decide if something is your calling.

Every time I hear a thought leader, guru, or expert advise people to find their passion I throw up a little, because they are setting folks up for failure and disappointment.

Passion is too high a bar, so give yourself a break. People use the P-word as if it's easy to find your life's calling. Ideally, they think this should happen before you're seventeen, preferably before you apply to college so you have something for your essay, and certainly before you're twenty.

In reality, it can take years to find your passion—indeed, "find" is the wrong word because it implies that once you find something, the process is over. Truly, you *develop* your passions—it's rarely love at first sight.

Passions start as "interests" that are acorns. And to use another nature metaphor, a butterfly is a caterpillar before it's a butterfly. You can't know what will take root, so you should pursue things that merely "interest" you. Some may develop into full-fledged passions over the course of your lifetime, but only because you planted many acorns, and some have taken root.

Build Random Connections

∠ You want to learn how to become a better networker in your everyday life, even during mundane situations.

∠ You're pondering how to decide which relationships are worth investing in.

∠ You want examples of how networking with random people can pay off.

One of the benefits of getting an education, pursuing interests, playing sports, and working for companies with good products is meeting more people. It's the law of big numbers: the more people you know, the more likely you'll develop meaningful relationships and make connections.

Here are three examples from my life (and podcast):

■ I became friends with Neil Pearlberg, who hosts the *Off the Lip* podcast, because we both surf at the same spot in Santa Cruz.

Figure 3.4   Brandi Chastain celebrates after kicking the game-winning goal in the 1999 World Cup final against China.

(Source: © Branimir Kvartuc/Zuma Press)

Through Neil, I was able to invite Leon Panetta, former Secretary of Defense; Chris Bertish, winner of the 2010 Mavericks Surf Contest; and Dave Ebert, shark expert, author, and TV personality to my podcast.

- A random encounter at the Apple Store in Santa Barbara, California, led to a fantastic connection. While I was at the Genius Bar getting my son's iPhone fixed, I met Shaun Tomson, a world champion surfer from the 1980s. The Apple "genius" had to explain to me who Shaun was!
- I was able to book Brandi Chastain, an Olympic and World Cup soccer player, for an interview. The connection was that Brandi is friends with John Conway, a divorce lawyer in Silicon Valley who has divided more estates in half than anyone I know. I met John while surfing in Santa Cruz too.

On the basis of this information, you could argue that the key to building random connections is surfing, and it would be difficult for me to refute that. But there are valuable underlying principles if you aren't a surfer:

- Smile. Few people want to meet, much less connect, with a grouch. A great smile involves more than just your mouth; it's the cheek-raising orbicularis oculi muscle that seals the deal. Search for the term "Duchenne smile" to learn more.
- Be curious. Ask what they do, where they work, and where they are from. The point is that open-ended questions require an extended response, not a simple yes or no, and catalyze a conversation.
- Let others talk too. A great conversation is a duet, not a monologue. It may seem illogical, but the best conversationalists listen more than they talk. (More about how to STFU later in this book if you need extra help in this area.)
- Be positive. A smile is the on ramp, but positivity is the fast lane to making random connections. Few people are looking for additional downers in their life, and almost everyone would like to know additional uplifting, positive people.

While surfing has its charm, building meaningful connections isn't confined to the ocean. You can make connections with any shared interest—from acrobatics to ziplining—that brings you into contact with people.

Make a genuine Duchenne smile, fuel conversations with curiosity, let others do the talking, and keep a positive vibe. These are your fast lanes to form random connections, no surfboard required.

Don't Be Picky

- ∠ You're wondering if you should swallow your pride or be picky about opportunities.
- ∠ You want to know if people can leverage humble first jobs into bigger things.
- ∠ You want to learn how to appreciate a placeholder job and utilize the skills obtained to go further.

There is no such thing as a placeholder job if you have a growth mindset! For example, listen to Derek Sivers, a musician, circus ring-leader, entrepreneur, programmer, author, and TED speaker, explain the start of his career:

> *I was seventeen years old, and my friend had an agent. His agent called him, and said, "Hey, there's a pig show that pays $75 for you to go play some strolling music. Will you do it?"*
>
> *. . . I didn't care that I was going to make a whopping $20 because this was my first paying gig ever. I was given really no instruction. Just get on this bus, go to this place.*
>
> *. . . I just walked around this pig show with a guitar on my neck just playing guitar. I got back on the bus to Boston, and then the agent called me, and said, "This is Greg Merrill. I heard you did a really good job at the pig show . . . . I want you to play at the art gallery opening. If you do well at the art opening, then you're in the circus."*
>
> *That's how I got my job in the circus, which ended up being over 1,000 shows. Eventually I started making $300 per show and performed 1,000 shows around the Northeast US. It was an amazing stage experience . . . .*
>
> *All of these things, such a massive experience, because I said yes to the $75 pig-show gig . . . . I just said yes to everything, which is a wonderful strategy early in your career.*

Pride and pickiness often prevent people from seizing opportunities. The overachiever's dream of graduating from an Ivy League university and jumping on the fast track at McKinsey or Goldman Sachs to fame and fortune on the way to "infinity and beyond" is unrealistic—and unremarkable, even if you pull it off.

None of the guests on my podcast followed this route; the majority of them started in entry-level positions and labored for years. It makes no difference where you begin or who assists you. What matters is your final destination.

Fight Framing

∠ You're wondering if you should focus on one interest or diversify to multiple ones.

Figure 3.5   Derek Sivers in a prior role to his tech and entrepreneurship career. He was the ringleader of a circus.

(Source: Tarleton Reynolds)

∠ You're curious about how skills from one interest can transfer and enhance other interests.

∠ You want to avoid external pressure to box you into predestined paths.

Two remarkable athletes, Brandi Chastain and Kerri Walsh Jennings, told me that kids should not specialize in a sport before graduating from high school. Brandi is the remarkable soccer player who won a gold medal in the 1996 Olympics and was on the 1991 and 1999 World Cup–winning teams.

Kerri Walsh Jennings, volleyball player, is a five-time Olympian and three-time gold medalist. She holds the record for tournament victories both domestically and internationally.

Figure 3.6   Kerri Walsh Jennings (right) and Misty May–Treanor at the medal ceremony of the London 2012 Olympic Games. They were the gold-medal team in women's beach volleyball.

(Source: Cameron Spencer/Getty Images)

Playing multiple sports can improve skills that apply across the board. Kerri, for example, wishes she played soccer for better footwork. The same advice applies to other activities, interests, and subjects too. Play the field and don't get put in a box too soon as a soccer player, volleyball player, secretary, or pig-show musician.

There is a pernicious form of framing called "ableism" that merits special attention. It's the act of exclusion and discrimination based on what you think a person is able to do. For example, you might believe that a deaf and blind person couldn't be a lawyer.

That's because you don't know Haben Girma. She is a deaf and blind graduate of Harvard Law School who works as a disability rights lawyer—to put it mildly, she is "otherwise enabled." Here is how she describes overcoming ableism:

> *Ableism is the widespread practice of framing disabled people as inferior to non-disabled people. So, for example, my disability does not stop me from*

practicing law. A big part of law is reading. I can read in Braille. Reading in Braille gives me access.

. . . I have not had to overcome my disability. I'm still disabled. I'm still deaf-blind. The biggest barrier for me has been ableism.

Remember how Beethoven inspired me? Haben is a hero too: If she can be blind and deaf and graduate from Harvard Law School and practice law, then I can be deaf and podcast. The lesson is: Do not let others—including yourself—define you.

Start in Sales

∠ You're wondering if a sales role is good training for your career development.

∠ You want to learn how to market yourself and your potential.

∠ You're curious if pursuing an intimidating position would help with the development of skills.

After graduating from the UCLA MBA program, I worked in sales and marketing for a fine-jewelry manufacturer. The company sold its products to jewelry stores, and this function was hand-to-hand combat—before sales became the act of testing button placement and colored text on web pages.

There are few functions as good as sales to force you to get outside your bubble and reach out to people you don't already know. Here's what you will learn:

- Patience. It will take a long time to get your foot in the door, to get an order, and to get paid. Few buyers operate on your ideal timetable.
- Resilience. Perhaps the most valuable lesson from starting in sales is learning to cope with constant rejection. There's no such thing as an easy sale, so you must keep trying.
- Persuasion. Once you get your foot in the door, you have to convince people to buy what you're selling, and that takes persuasion.

You will be selling for the rest of your life, or at least a significant portion of it, so you should strive to become skilled at it. Sales include applying for a job, requesting a date, obtaining a promotion, raising money, and scheduling an appointment—valuable real-world skills.

Make Yourself Indispensable

∠ You want to make the most of an internship by learning how to focus on personal development.

∠ You need help setting a goal for an internship experience.

∠ You're wondering how to start your career with a bang.

Andrew Zimmern, TV star and master of meals, menus, and meringue, told me a great way to grow from seed to seedling. He was given this advice by his mentor and spiritual guru after securing the unpaid internship at a television station in Minnesota:

Make yourself indispensable.

Come on down, Andrew, you are today's recipient of the *Remarkable People* Award in the category of Most Remarkable Career Advice. When you're an unpaid intern at three different places and you get job offers from all of them, you're doing things the right way.

These are the ways to become an indispensable asset to your company and boss:

- Show up. Indispensable people show up and do the work. Dispensable people don't. It's that simple. It makes no difference whether this takes place in real life or online.
- Do what nobody else wants to do. Doing whatever is necessary, no matter how unappealing, is a great way to show that you are valuable and to separate yourself from the pack.
- Broaden your skill set. The more skills you have, the more you can do. And the more you can do, the more valuable you are.
- Own a niche. The ability to do something few people can do is valuable too. Imagine if you're the only person who can edit video at a television station.

Figure 3.7   Andrew Zimmern using some "lucky chopsticks" at the South Beach Wine and Food Festival in Miami, Florida, 2016.

(Source: Aaron Davidson / Getty Images)

- Establish high standards. Your best effort should be applied to all of your endeavors. Being merely adequate and "good enough" is insufficient if you wish to be remarkable.
- Make your boss look good. If your boss looks good, you look good. If your boss does well, you do well. Your professional lives are intertwined. Making your boss look bad is never going to help you.

I can just imagine Andrew showing up early; doing the shit work of cleaning sets; learning how to do makeup, sound, lighting, and guest booking; and mastering a niche like programming teleprompters—all at the highest level, which made his boss look good.

This guidance will be helpful to you in both your personal and your professional lives, and it may even be useful to you in the afterlife (I believe in karma). People who are indispensable to others are almost always remarkable.

Weed the Seeds

∠ You want to figure out who to believe.

∠ You want to learn when to listen and when to speak.

∠ You want insight into the necessity of a college education.

Remember how I had to weed out the dead acorns by seeing which ones sank and which one floated? You need to similarly qualify the data and information that you encounter.

This process is called discernment. It is the ability to make wise judgments—to see the difference between what is true and what is false, what is good and what is bad, what is important and what is not.

Here's how to apply the process of discernment to the data and information that's coming at you:

- **Assess yourself.** How much do you know about the topic? Are you already biased in a certain direction? The less you know and the more biased you are, the more you should shut up and listen.
- **Read laterally.** My buddy Sam Wineburg, emeritus professor of education at Stanford, taught me to stop reading only an organization's website. You need to get off the site and read "laterally" across multiple sources such as Wikipedia and Google News.
- **Assess the sources.** What is the basis of the knowledge and opinions of the sources? Is it academic training, real-world experience, or wishful thinking? Do the sources have good track records?
- **Survey consensus.** Is there agreement among multiple expert sources about the topic? You may have a contrarian view, but it's good to know if there is a predomination of opinion. As my mother used to tell me, "When three people tell you you're drunk, you take a cab."
- **Assess transparency.** Is the motivation of the sources out in the open? Are there conflicts of interest and hidden agendas that are influencing the information? Do they explain their data, methodology, and reasoning, or do they require leaps of faith?

- Examine the sequence. First, did the effect happen *after* the supposed cause? Second, even if the sequence is right, is there a plausible relationship between cause and effect? Steve Jobs didn't finish college, but that's not what made him remarkable.

Discernment skills will help you decide when to listen, when to ignore, and when to challenge. Mastering them makes the process of growth more efficient. And one more ultra-powerful tip: imagine that you are being discerned rather than doing the discerning. How do you stack up?

Figure 3.8   A scene from the "invisible gorilla" experiment. Fifty percent of the subjects watching the video did not notice the gorilla who appeared for nine seconds.

(Source: Daniel Simons et al., 1999 / SAGE PUBLICATIONS, INC.)

Ask, "What's Missing?"

Here's another simple but powerful (and seldom used) discernment skill: ask, "What's missing?" I learned this technique from Dan Simons, professor of psychology at the University of Illinois. He's the guy who did the "invisible gorilla" video.

Dan told me that many authors and experts delight in telling the story of Steve Jobs (Reed College, 1972), Bill Gates (Harvard University, 1975), and Mark Zuckerberg (Harvard University, 2004) dropping out of college but still succeeding.

This is the time-honored tradition of studying successful people or companies and then labeling what they share as the cause of their success. In this case, the implications are that dropouts make great entrepreneurs, and a college education isn't necessary to succeed.

However, Dan's co-author, Chris Chabris, found that in 2015 all the CEOs of the 253 "unicorns" (private companies with a valuation of at least $1 billion) had college degrees. And this is a snapshot of only 2015, whereas the cherry-picked example of Jobs, Gates, and Zuckerberg spans decades.

If you consider only the handful of highly successful entrepreneurs without college degrees, what's missing is the fact that there are far more successful entrepreneurs who have college degrees. Maybe it's a good idea to get a college degree after all . . . .

Learn to think in a two-by-two matrix format to understand the whole picture. Note that even with the information from Chabris, we don't have all the information!

	Not successful	Successful
No college degree	Unknown!	Jobs, Gates, Zuckerberg
College degree	Unknown!	Unicorn CEOs

When presented with facts, always ask, "What's missing?" If you ignore the dropout-turn-billionaire examples, you will discover that most successful tech CEOs have degrees. The key takeaway is always to consider what overlooked facts may contradict the story being told.

Additional Resources

- Girma, Haben. *Haben: The Deafblind Woman Who Conquered Harvard Law.*
- Goodall, Jane. *Reason for Hope: A Spiritual Journey.*
- Isaacson, Walter. *Steve Jobs* (must be a good book—it doesn't even need a subtitle).
- Simons, Daniel. *Nobody's Fool: Why We Get Taken in and What We Can Do About It.*
- Simons, Daniel, and Chabris, Christopher. *The Invisible Gorilla: And Other Ways Our Intuitions Deceive Us.*
- Wineburg, Sam. *How to Think Straight, Get Duped Less, and Make Better Decisions About What to Believe Online.*
- Wineburg, Sam. *Why Learn History (When It's Already on Your Phone).*
- Zimmern, Andrew. *The Bizarre Truth: How I Walked out the Door Mouth First . . . and Came Back Shaking My Head.*

STAGE 2

Grit—Activate Your Aspirations

4 | Do Good Shit

Problem plus hope equals change.

—Olivia Julianna

Embrace the Grit Mindset

∠ You want to understand what grit is.
∠ You're wondering if grit is necessary to succeed.
∠ You want to learn how to adopt a gritty mindset.

This chapter is called "Do Good Shit" because there is no better way to describe what your goal should be. Good shit can be a product, service, team, classroom, group, art, sports, or a life—this is up to you.

But this is what we've been preparing for this whole time. Doing good shit takes resilience, perseverance, and patience—aka grit. Angela Duckworth is a professor at the University of Pennsylvania, MacArthur Fellow, and grit evangelist. She wrote the book on the subject: *Grit: The Power of Passion and Perseverance*.

Let's start with how she defines grit:

> *Grit is about having what some researchers call an "ultimate concern"—a goal you care about so much that it organizes and gives meaning to almost*

everything you do. And grit is holding steadfast to that goal. Even when you
fall down. Even when you screw up. Even when progress toward that goal is
halting or slow.

You don't wake up one morning and decide to be gritty. It's a mindset that causes changes in your behavior. It starts with an interest in something. You decide to pursue this interest and to learn more.

After the initial attraction wears off, you continue the work. You seek coaching and support. You find examples of gritty people to inspire you. Failure along the way makes you try harder. You realize that innate "talent" or lack of it doesn't determine success or failure. Even if you change interests, the grit mindset remains and transfers to other activities.

You surround yourself with people who have similar levels of determination and resilience. You put in hours and hours of work. Instead of forcing yourself to be gritty, you cannot stop being gritty. This work ethic defines your existence.

Eventually you get so good that you want to help others who share the same interest. What started as an interest has become a calling (remember the word *ikigai,* which we'll explore in the next chapter) and a way to make a difference.

Grit is the most important four-letter word in the English language for a person trying to be remarkable. It is a characteristic shared by all remarkable people. You show me a person with grit, and I'll show you someone who is remarkable.

Create What You Want to Use

- ∠ You want to learn how people come up with ideas for products and services.
- ∠ You're looking for validation of curiosity, tinkering, and experimenting.
- ∠ You're wondering if something you made for yourself could be commercially viable.

The application of grit starts with pursuing an interest. It means visualizing a change that you want to make—in yourself or with a product, service, book, piece of art, or cause. The remainder of this chapter describes how to visualize change.

Let's start with an example from my past. Steve Jobs didn't design the first Apple computer. Steve Wozniak did. Woz created the computer that he wanted to use, and luckily for both Steves and for the world, Woz wasn't the only person who wanted a personal computer.

Mike Moritz of Sequoia Capital, perhaps the greatest venture capitalist ever (Google, Yahoo!, PayPal, LinkedIn, Zappos, Dropbox, WhatsApp), once told me that the richest vein for tech startups is nerds building what they want to use. It isn't being "market driven" unless you consider yourself a market of one.

The "creating what you want to use" method wasn't invented or perfected by tech nerds. One of my favorite old-school, low-tech examples is Bette Nesmith Graham, who invented Liquid Paper ("white out") in the early 1950s.

Bette was a secretary in a Texas bank and wanted a way to correct her typing mistakes. She experimented with various paints and soap and then added titanium dioxide to her formulas. The concoction covered up mistakes completely, and soon other secretaries asked her for her correction fluid.

We hear more about the ideas that succeeded and less about the ideas that failed (remember to think about what's missing). But when you create something for yourself, there is at least one person who desires it, and you are in the game. So method number one to visualize change is to make what you want to use.

Alleviate Pain

- ∠ You're wondering if alleviating pain is a viable business strategy.
- ∠ You know some people who are in pain and would like to figure out a way to help them.
- ∠ You want to use your own story of pain to reduce pain in others.

Eliminating suffering from people's lives is an excellent means of achieving remarkableness. As a migraine sufferer, I can tell you that people are tremendously motivated by pain and are appreciative when it's reduced.

Here are three examples of remarkable people who have alleviated pain for a large number of beneficiaries.

Name	Organization	Pain Alleviated
Melanie Perkins	Canva	Expense and difficulty of graphic design
Marc Benioff	Salesforce	Updating software in the field for millions of people
Gretchen Carlson	Lift Our Voices	Sexual harassment in the workplace

Ask yourself, "Whose pain can I alleviate?" to uncover opportunities. When people are in pain, they are typically eager, if not desperate,

Figure 4.1   Gretchen Carlson shaking hands with President Joe Biden while Vice President Kamala Harris applauds, 2022. They are celebrating the signing of H.R. 4445, the "Ending Forced Arbitration of Sexual Assault and Sexual Harassment Act of 2021."

(Source: Anna Moneymaker/Getty Images)

for relief. You could be on the path to remarkableness if you can identify people's pain and create solutions for them.

Work Backwards

∠ You're wondering if you should focus on what you like to do or what customers want.

∠ You'd like to turn insights into new product development.

∠ You are curious about the correct approach to creating a valuable product.

According to Colin Bryar, former chief of staff of the founder and CEO of Amazon, one of the keys to Amazon's success was the practice of creating new products and services by working backwards from what customers wanted instead of forward from what a company has been doing, likes to do, or wants to do.

Netflix is an example of working backwards. CEO Reed Hastings realized that people wanted to watch a wide selection of movies without having to drive to a Blockbuster store. The first permutation of Netflix involved mailing DVDs to customers, but Hastings must always have intended to use the Internet—even though this was when download speeds were not yet high enough to do this—since the company's name started with "Net" from day one.

Vans, the shoe company, is another example. Early in its life, a woman walked into a Vans store with a piece of pink fabric looking to find shoes to match the dress she made. None of the shoes in the store worked, but Vans founder Paul Van Doren offered to make shoes from the leftover fabric.

This led to outfitting many Southern California cheerleading and sports teams who also wanted shoes that matched their outfits. Van Doren also instituted a policy to allow only one shoe to be sold to customers in case only one got lost or damaged (because skateboarders tend to wear out one shoe before the other).

Most organizations work in the opposite direction: "This is what we do, this is what we like to do, and this is what we are good at doing. We just need to get customers to do business our way." Blockbuster's attitude was probably, "We have stores where people come to rent movies." Shoe manufacturers made limited styles in large quantities and always sold them in pairs.

If you work forward from your skills and interests, you must hope that you are addressing a genuine need. By contrast, if you start with people's needs and work backwards, you are more assured that they will embrace what you're doing.

Resolve Your Indignation

∠ You want to know if being pissed off can be turned into constructive motivation.

∠ You need examples of organizations that started as a way to righting wrongs.

∠ You want to learn how to tap indignation as a creative force.

Addressing something that pisses you off is a good way to identify a cause, as is righting wrongs even if they don't directly affect you. Chances are that you aren't alone in your feelings, and others appreciate and support what you're doing.

Think of the people who fight pollution, climate change, and crime. Here are three more examples of activation by indignation:

Organization	Motivation
Mothers Against Drunk Driving	Lenient sentence of the drunk driver who killed Candace Lightner's daughter
Mothers Against Greg Abbott ("MAGA," get it?)	Children put in harm's way by Texas Governor Greg Abbott's policies
Black Lives Matter	Systemic racism and violence against Black people

Mothers Against Greg Abbott started August 6, 2021, because Nancy Thompson was indignant that the Texas Education Agency ended the COVID mask mandate and issued wimpy "guidance."

Figure 4.2   Nancy Thompson with her MAGA sign at the start of the Mothers Against Greg Abbott movement, August 2021.

She created a poster board with two Sharpies, one blue and one red, and drove to the state capitol building to protest Texas's limp COVID prevention efforts, failure to strengthen the power grid, and the reduction of women's and LGBTQ+ rights.

Nancy posted a picture of her protest to Facebook and Twitter. Passersby took her picture and posted to their social media too. A week later, a protest of one had increased to a movement of thousands.

Anger or annoyance prompted by unfairness or injustice can motivate extraordinary responses and motivate people to seek solutions. This sequence of events has prompted numerous individuals to rise up and make a difference for the benefit of society.

Jump to the Next Curve

∠ You're wondering if it's better to tap an existing market or create a new market.

∠ You're worried about your product or service becoming irrelevant.

∠ You'd like insights into innovation by incremental improvements versus leapfrogs.

Jumping to the next curve or creating the next curve means that you are creating the future rather than reacting to it. A classic example is the ice business: it went from *ice harvesting* from frozen ponds to *ice factories* that froze water anywhere at any time of year to *refrigerators*, personal ice factories in people's homes.

Apple transformed computers by jumping curves. It went from character-based computers (Apple I and II) to graphical-user interface computers (Macintosh and Lisa), to a portable music player (iPod), to a portable tablet (iPad), to a smartphone (iPhone). There are few companies that created or jumped so many curves, and that's what makes Apple remarkable.

Figure 4.3   Steve Sasson and the first digital camera ever made. He worked for Kodak at the time, 1975.

Kodak is the mother of bad examples of this concept. In 1970, a Kodak engineer named Steven Sasson invented the digital camera. His invention weighed eight pounds and had a resolution of 100×100 pixels. (An iPhone 14 weighs six ounces and has a resolution of 8064×6048 pixels.)

Unfortunately, Kodak lived, thrived, and then died on the film curve. In case you don't know what film is, it's a sheet of plastic covered with chemicals that "capture" a picture when exposed to light. Once exposed, you would take your roll of film to a lab or drugstore for processing. In as little as an hour or as long as a few days, you could have prints of your pictures.

Kodak did not embrace the next curve, digital photography, even though the company invented it. Maybe Kodak thought it was a chemical and film company, and to be fair, it would have been difficult to make that eight-pound prototype into a consumer device.

I would guess things didn't go well when Steve told his management that he invented a product to make the company's current products unnecessary! This is a classic example of a fixed mindset. Kodak apparently defined its business as a packager of film and chemicals—that's what it did, the business was lucrative, and it wasn't going to change.

If it defined its business as the preservation of memories and jumped the curve from chemicals to digital chips, we might be using Kodak cameras today, and its technology would be in every phone. In other words, what Sony is, circa 2023.

My observation is that truly innovative and remarkable businesses develop products that accelerate the next curve. On the current curve, there are few advancements; instead, the competition is for mindshare and market share. The next turn is where the action is.

Ride the Tide

∠ You're wondering whether it's better to be too early or too late for a trend.

∠ You want to jump on a big trend that's already rocking and rolling.

∠ You want to learn to work toward what is an apparent, increasing need.

Sometimes the next curve is already forming. Then the recommendation is to seek ways to "raise the tide" for everyone—not only your boat. For example, back in the 1970s, establishing the viability of personal computers was good not only for Apple but for Commodore, IBM, and Compaq too.

It means that someone else's gain is not necessarily your loss, and that your loss is not necessarily their gain. Everyone can succeed on a tide that's rising. More examples of the power of a rising tide include:

- Car companies that used internal combustion engines rode the electric-car tide. Tesla created that tide, and the rest benefited.
- Zoom rode the tide of working remotely when the pandemic struck in 2020. The demand for digital communications was a tsunami.
- Shopify benefited from the digitization of retailing. When people could no longer shop in person, retailers created massive demand for online stores that Shopify tapped.

Do not misunderstand: the leading edge of remarkableness is to be the first to jump curves and create the tide, but you can also achieve remarkableness by riding a rising tide. That's what's known in Silicon Valley as being a "fast second," which entails the benefits and thrills of being the innovator but with less risk.

Go See, Go Be, and Go Do

∠ You want to learn ways to understand customer needs.
∠ You want to optimize your development process.
∠ You wish to adopt and utilize compassion as a result of empathy.

Toyota extols the principle of *genchi genbutsu* (go and see for yourself). For Toyota that means that one should go and see what's happening on the factory floor, in car dealers, and in the lives of customers as they use cars.

This process helps you gain an appreciation of what people are experiencing to improve their lives—for example, seeing how a young family deals with a baby, a stroller, a dog, and siblings influenced the design of Toyota's minivans.

Even better than going and seeing is the concept of *taiken gakushu* (experiential learning). Doing or participating is the way to learn. For example, Chiesi Farmaceutici asked Martin Lindstrom, Norwegian psychologist and executive leader, to help the company "get closer to the customer."

Usually this involves focus groups and surveys. Instead, he assembled the executives in a room and made them breathe through straws. Many executives had difficulty doing it for more than a few minutes.

At the end of exercise, Martin asked the participants if they now understood what it's like to be a someone with asthma. These executives didn't simply go see or imagine themselves as asthmatic. They *experienced* what it's like to have asthma.

Figure 4.4   Martin Lindstrom discussing the lessons of breathing through straws with the staff of Chiesi Pharmaceutical, 2019. This was a powerful way for the employees to understand what it's like to live with asthma.

(Source: Martin Lindstrom)

Another "go and be" story: When Temple Grandin, professor, animal behaviorist, and visual thinker, was a graduate student at Arizona State University, she figured out why cattle would balk at walking through chutes. While the ranch hands resorted to prodding, pushing, and yelling, she got down into the chute and "became" a cow. She saw the shadows, rays of light, and distractions to understand what made the cows hesitate. *Yellowstone* fans, I ask you, "Doesn't this seem like something John Dutton would do?"

"Go and see" and "go and be" foster the ability to feel what other people (or animals!) are feeling. This is a good practice. However, being remarkable also requires making the leap from empathy to action. The desire to relieve what's causing suffering is called compassion.

For example, it's great that you now realize how difficult it is for people with asthma to breath, but what are you going to do about it? Empathy is a visceral reaction. Compassion is a conscious action.

To quote Jordan Kassalow, the author of *Dare to Matter: Your Path to Making a Difference*, "Now, while empathy can exhaust us, compassion nourishes us. It does not cost us anything. The more we contribute, the more it will grow." So three paths to remarkableness are to go see, go be, and go do.

Do the Right Thing

∠ You are wondering if doing the right thing is a path to making a difference.

∠ You're looking for a modern example of doing the right thing.

∠ You'd like insights into the costs of doing the right thing.

Another path to being remarkable involves a different kind of doing. In this case, doing something at great personal risk, cost, and sacrifice can lead to remarkableness. For example, Tyler Shultz blew the whistle on Elizabeth Holmes and Sunny Balwani, the dynamic duo from Theranos who were convicted of defrauding investors and customers.

When Shultz saw that Theranos's product was ineffective while Holmes and Balwani were continuing to promote it, he took the high road and informed the *Wall Street Journal* and a medical regulator.

Figure 4.5 Bill Clinton and Elizabeth Holmes on stage at the 2015 plenary session of the Clinton Global Initiative, when people still believed the Theranos product worked.

(Source: Taylor Hill/Getty Images)

This cost him two years of his life, $750,000 in legal fees, and his relationship with his grandfather, George Shultz, Theranos board member and former US secretary of state.

The obvious question is whether he would do it again. This is what he told me:

It's an interesting question because when people first started asking me that question when I was twenty-six years old, shortly after, or while I was still really in it, my answer was, "No way, I would never do this again. It was totally not worth it."

And as more and more time has passed, I'm starting to see more the positives that have come out of it, and now that the threats are totally gone, I really have been able to turn this really terrible negative experience into a positive experience.

. . . I speak to tons of universities and classes, and at conferences, and I really get a lot out of those types of events. I'm always having people coming up to me afterwards saying, "I was in a very similar situation and your story inspired me to do the right thing," and that means a lot to me, it really does.

Often, doing the right thing is neither the simplest nor the most practical option. Nonetheless, making a difference may be the light at the end of the tunnel. Pay attention to your inner compass and denounce dishonesty and fraud, but also recognize that this course involves personal risk.

Transform Yourself

∠ You want to learn how to transform your own life despite obstacles and hardships.

∠ You want to show people that overcoming obstacles is not impossible.

∠ You believe that where you end up is more important than where you started.

Transformation of your own life is another path to being remarkable and making a difference. It underlies the remarkable accomplishment of people overcoming hardship such as Martha Niño, a woman who was smuggled across the US border as a baby in 1975.

Martha's family came from Pueblo Viejo, Zacatecas, Mexico (population 300), to the United States, seeking a better life. They settled in California, working various jobs while living in a one-bedroom duplex. Martha attended school and worked to support her family. A guidance counselor at her school helped her balance work and school, allowing her to graduate on time.

Martha worked in warehouses, furniture manufacturing, and then at tech companies such as Creative Labs and Handspring. Observing her colleagues' career advancements because of college degrees, she completed her degree at the University of Phoenix. A short time later Martha joined Adobe, a graphics software company, as a temporary contractor in 2003.

Figure 4.6 Martha Niño and her mother, Tomasa Coloa, at the Niles Flea Market in Fremont, California, 2023.

(Source: Raul Ceja)

By 2023, she emerged as a leader at Adobe, authored a book titled *The Other Side: From a Shack to Silicon Valley,* and became an activist for diversity and inclusion. What a remarkable success story! She was Adobe's first student engagement community leader.

The story of Martha's transformation from an undocumented immigrant to a tech executive is an example of personal transformation. It required the sacrifice and tenacity of her parents, assistance from mentors, her own efforts, workable immigration laws, and good fortune. The point is that remarkable personal transformations are possible.

Ask Simple Questions

- ∠ You want to know if questioning conventional wisdom is wisdom.
- ∠ You want to create simple solutions to common problems by beginning with the basics.
- ∠ You're seeking validation of the value of innocence and naivete as avenues for insights.

Remarkable people don't usually start with grandiose plans of crushing or dominating the universe. They start with small and simple questions that over time yield the result of making a difference:

- Isn't this strange? Scientists at Pfizer developed a drug for heart problems and noticed that men seem to get improved erections because of it.
- Is there a better way? Edwin Land's daughter asked him why she had to wait to see the photographs that he had taken. Land went on to found Polaroid, the instant-camera company.
- Why has no one done this before? Salesforce answers a simple question: "Why do software updates require manual installation at each location?"

I don't know if people asked these exact questions at Pfizer, Polaroid, and Salesforce, but I do know that simple questions like these foster three processes:

- Identify assumptions that represent gaps and flaws in the status quo.
- Encourage a broader range of curiosity and collaboration.
- Reframe how people view problems by simplifying complicated issues.

In order for simple questions to be effective, these conditions are necessary:

- People must feel free to ask unconventional questions and provide divergent responses without fear of ridicule or retribution.
- The questions must be motivated by genuine curiosity and the desire to comprehend and gain knowledge by delving deeper and investigating further.
- Individuals must be receptive to all potential responses and be willing to listen, learn, and adapt in unanticipated ways.

Don't accept that what everyone "knows is true" is true. Primatologists thought they "knew" that chimps were vegetarians with limited social interactions, and they believed that only humans have the intelligence to create and use tools.

This appeared true until Jane Goodall went to Gombe, Nigeria, and witnessed chimps eating meat, fighting, and using tools. "How do you know chimps aren't social?" she simply asked the experts.

As the Bible says, "Out of the mouth of babes and sucklings hast thou ordained strength." Posing questions that lack guile and come from a place of innocence, naiveite, or candidness is a rich vein for ideas to make the world a better place.

Establish a Subcategory

∠ You want insights into defining a niche as a low-cost way to market your product or service.

∠ You'd like to figure out ways to position your competition to your advantage.

∠ You're torn between the strategies of going deep or going broad.

David Aaker, the godfather of branding, advises that creating an entirely new category is often too hard and too late. Establishing a subcategory is remarkable enough.

Here are examples:

Category	Subcategory	Example
Cars	Electric	Tesla
Cameras	Action	GoPro
Tablets	E-reader	Kindle

And here are the reasons to focus on creating a subcategory instead of a new category:

■ It's cheaper to create a niche within a category because people have a basic understanding of what you do. It is easier to explain a Kindle e-reader as a subcategory of tablets than as a totally new market.

- You can target groups with unique needs and requirements. This helps you focus your efforts and easily ignore other segments. GoPro, for example, doesn't have to worry about serving wedding photographers unless wingsuit weddings suddenly takes off.

- You can redefine and reposition your competitors. For example, an electric-car company can label its internal combustion competitors as brands that don't care about the environment.

- While you cannot discourage competitors in a large, generic market, by creating a subcategory you can encourage them to leave you alone. Have you heard of action cameras made by Sony, Canon, Leica, or Nikon? That's because they all leave GoPro alone.

Creating a new category is a remarkable accomplishment, but new categories are rare. You can make a difference without completing this monumental endeavor. I want you to envision yourself as a large fish in a large pond, and this you can do by starting with a subcategory.

Get Unique and Valuable

∠ You need a framework to understand how to differentiate your product or service.

∠ You seek a way to evaluate the competitive landscape.

∠ You're wondering what messages your marketing should focus on.

A good test of the viability of an idea is whether it is both unique and valuable. Unique means people cannot get it from other organizations. Valuable means that it is worth getting at all.

	Not Unique	Unique
Valuable	Brutal price competition	Remarkable!
Not Valuable	Total loser	Solution in search of a problem

When something is not unique, it's difficult to set yourself off from the pack. And when something isn't valuable, well, why bother doing it at all?

Joe Foster, the founder of Reebok, calls this "whitespace." He told me that the company "arrived in America as a running company." But then an employee named Angel Martinez saw that his wife was loving classes where people were "exercising to music."

Angel went to the next class and saw the instructor and half the students in sneakers. The other half was not wearing shoes. This inspired Angel to want to make aerobics shoes for women. Angel got 200 samples made, and they sold immediately.

Angel had helped Reebok develop a product that was unique and valuable—filling a profitable whitespace because no other company was making shoes for women to wear while doing aerobics. And then Jane Fonda wore a pair and helped propel Reebok from a $9 million company into a $900 million company.

Here are more recent and high-tech examples of unique and valuable products in their time.

Figure 4.7 Reebok got "unique and valuable" in 1982 with the introduction of the Reebok Freestyle model. It was the only shoe designed for aerobics and helped Reebok enter the mainstream athletic wear market.

(Source: ReebokUSA/Wikimedia Commons/CC BY-SA 4.0)

iPod	The only device with a user interface that a mortal could understand that could carry thousands of songs.
Netflix	The only way to get a broad array of movies without driving to a store.
Waze	The only GPS system that offered real-time traffic reports and optimized routes.

When what you're offering is unique and valuable, then marketing, selling, fundraising, and recruiting all get easier—it is the holy grail, and promised land of innovation, so do your best to create products and services that embody both qualities.

Additional Resources

- Fadell, Tony. *Build: An Unorthodox Guide to Making Things Worth Making.*
- Grandin, Temple. *Visual Thinking: The Hidden Gifts of People Who Think in Pictures, Patterns, and Abstractions.*
- Niño, Martha. *The Other Side: From a Shack to Silicon Valley.*
- Pinker, Steven. *Enlightenment Now: The Case for Reason, Science, Humanism, and Progress.*
- Rubin, Rick. *The Creative Act: A Way of Being.*
- Van Doren, Paul. *Authentic: A Memoir by the Founder of Vans.*

5 | Get Beyond Eureka

As we move beyond the joy of having a great idea, our Eureka! moment, we soon realize that we have entered a realm of uncertainty.

—Maryléne Delbourg-Delphis

Formalize Your Goals

∠ You wonder if formalizing your objectives is a worthwhile endeavor.

∠ You want to know whether the most challenging aspect of making an impact is idea generation or implementation.

∠ You want to maximize the efficiency and effectiveness of implementing your idea.

"Eureka" is an expression that means "I have found it." People use it to communicate feelings of excitement and triumph when they solve a problem or make a discovery. However, the term is often used prematurely—as if coming up with the ideas is the hard part. In the real world, ideas are easy, and implementation is hard.

For example, "Eureka, we can use real-world images like trash cans, folders, and icons. Then more people can understand how to use a computer." That's wonderful, but now you need to design the computer, build it in large quantities, and get people to buy it.

Formalizing your goals by writing them down helps you to go beyond Eureka and achieve results. Garrett McNamara, my humongous-wave surfer buddy, explains what people do wrong:

> We just go day by day. We have these visions or dreams or hopes or expectations, but we don't really write it on a paper. We don't really make a roadmap to achieve it.
>
> So we aimlessly wander all day . . . what's coming next? And maybe we'll plan for the next day or plan for the next week, or even plan for the next month. But it's just usually day to day.
>
> It's not the big picture. How do I become an amazing human? How do I contribute? How do I feed my family and do what I love?

This is what Garrett thinks we should do instead:

> Make the plan of that and focus on that every day. Look at that roadmap every day—then you have a life of purpose. You know what you're doing. You know why you're doing it. You know what you can do to improve.

Writing down and formalizing your goals forces you to develop and analyze them more carefully. Watching them flow out of your brain onto a piece of paper or even a computer screen makes them more real, adds to their merit, and increases your commitment to complete them.

I'll give you the time and space to write down the three most important goals that you want to accomplish in the next year. Then come back to this page in a year when you've hopefully gone from believer to builder.

1.

2.

3.

Prove Your Concept

∠ You want to progress from imagining something to creating it.

∠ You're wondering what a "proof of concept" is.

∠ You need some way to help people understand your ideas.

The goal of proving your concept is what education guru Ken Robinson calls "the transition from imagination to creation." People have watched his TED Talk called *Do Schools Kill Creativity?* over sixty million times, and Queen Elizabeth II knighted him for his work. This is how he explained the process to me:

> *Imagination is the capacity we all have, we're born with it as human beings, to bring into mind things that aren't present to our senses. To transcend the here and now, to anticipate the future, to reflect on the past, to step outside, to speculate, to ask, "What if?"*
>
> *It's not a single power. It's an amalgam of many powers that we have, but the ability to bring to mind things that aren't present is the root of it. Creativity is a step on from that. It's putting your imagination to work. It's applying it in some specific way.*

The rest of this chapter explains how to make the transition from concept to concrete in the realm of uncertainty. It's a difficult, daunting, and sometimes depressing process, but this is the challenge that you have to overcome to make a difference and to be remarkable.

The first step is to create a proof of concept. This refers to a prototype or mockup that allows people to touch, feel, and interact with your idea. Even for the most gifted storyteller, it is difficult to help people visualize an idea. Proof of concepts varies between industries and markets.

The most perilous proof of concept that I've heard of was by Chris Bertish. He's the first person to paddle solo across the Atlantic Ocean. It took him ninety-three days, and he was self-sufficient without a support boat.

His proof of concept that such an endeavor was possible was a solo paddle from Cape Point to Lambert's Bay, a 350-kilometer

Figure 5.1   Chris Bertish arriving in Antigua in March 2017. His 4,600-mile journey took ninety-three days, and he was unassisted during the record-setting trip.

(Source: Brian Overfelt)

(217-mile) journey through shark-infested, cold, and turbulent waters along the west coast of South Africa.

Here are more mundane examples of proof of concept:

Industry	Proof of Concept
Biotech	Early-stage clinical trials
Automotive	Concept car
Television	Pilot episode

There's a saying in Silicon Valley that a prototype is worth a thousand slides. When it comes to getting beyond Eureka, there are few more powerful and useful tools than a proof of concept to make the transition from concept to concrete.

Get Mentors

∠ You want to learn about the importance of mentors.

∠ You need help finding mentors.

∠ You're wondering how to get the most out of a mentor relationship.

Margaret O'Mara, author of *The Code: Silicon Valley and the Remaking of America*, and an expert in the history of tech, told me that mentors were a big reason for the success of tech entrepreneurs who started in garages.

So I searched through the 4,000 pages of *Remarkable People* transcripts to find instances where guests acknowledge a "mentor." I had to stop at page 500 because there were already too many to use. Here is a partial list of remarkable people and their mentors.

Remarkable Person	Remarkable Mentor
Jamia Wilson: Feminist activist and book editor; author of *Young, Gifted, and Black,* plus nine other books	Gloria Steinem: Feminist icon and journalist, founder of *Ms.* magazine
Leana Wen: Physician, public health expert, former medical commissioner of Baltimore health department	Elijah Cummings: Civil rights activist and member of Congress, 1996–2019
Ronnie Lott: Ten-time Pro Bowl football player, eight-time All Pro, and four-time Super Bowl winner	Jim Brown: Professional football player, actor, and activist; considered the greatest running back of all time
Roy Yamaguchi: Pioneer of Hawaiian fusion cuisine; founder of Roy's Restaurants	Joseph Amendola: Chef and author of *Understanding Baking: The Art and Science of Baking*

Figure 5.2   Jamia Wilson with her mentor, Gloria Steinem, at a Harvard Book Store event in 2015. Steinem and Jamia appeared "in conversation" for Steinem's book *My Life on the Road*.

(Source: Dr. Willa Afreda Campbell-Wilson)

The message is clear: mentors are force multipliers. They can help you see opportunities, avoid mistakes, and stay on the right path. I asked Chandrika Tandon how to get a mentor. She should know because she grew up in a village in Chenai, India, and progressed to become the first Indian American female partner at McKinsey and Company, a Grammy-nominated musician, and a board member of Lincoln Center for Performing Arts.

She attributes much of her success to her mentors, and this is her advice on how to get mentors:

People will very openly and actively and energetically mentor you if you have done something good for them. There's something that they have to see.

Figure 5.3   Leana Wen with her mentor, Congressman Elijah Cummings, in Baltimore, 2018.

(Source: Leana Wen)

Mentors of mine were mostly my teachers. I really worked very hard in their classes. They remembered what I did in their classes. I did very, very well in school, but it wasn't only that I was academically good. I just took on a lot of jobs at school.

You don't just walk into somebody and say, "Oh, please be my mentor." You have to do something. Go beyond your call of duty.

Once you pay your dues and are able to get a mentor, then here's how to optimize the relationship for both of you.

- Look for tough love. You want someone who will challenge you to do the right things the right way and call you on your bullshit.
- Specify your needs. Don't make them try to figure out what you want from them. Be upfront and succinct. This demonstrates

Figure 5.4   Ronnie Lott and his mentor, Jim Brown, celebrating Jim's eightieth birthday, 2016.

(Source: Joe Scarnici / Getty Images)

    seriousness and thoughtfulness, which improves the likelihood of an affirmative response.

- Don't waste their time. The most valuable resource of all is time, so when you interact with your mentor, get your act together and know exactly what help you want. They are your mentors, not your psychiatrists.
- Listen to their feedback. If you want people to help you, don't spend time trying to convince them that they are wrong, or you already know a better way. Again, don't waste their time. It's their most precious resource.

Figure 5.5   Roy Yamaguchi with his mentor Joseph Amendola

(Source: Roy Yamaguchi)

■ Show your appreciation. Appreciation could be as simple as a handwritten note or a shoutout on social media. Certainly reciprocating by helping them in some way is effective.

It is difficult to find the right people and convince them to mentor you. However, it's safe to say that behind every remarkable person is probably a force-multiplying mentor that played a valuable role. Remember to do something to impress potential mentors and then utilize them well.

Find Complements

∠ You need to enhance your capabilities by identifying your weaknesses.

∠ You seek methods for discovering "force multipliers."

∠ You want to learn techniques to divide and overcome challenges.

In July 2023, Madisun and I had lunch with the "the shark guy," Dave Ebert. He's the author of numerous books about sharks, discoverer of more than sixty new species, and a TV personality. He regaled us with story after story of studying sharks in South Africa, Sri Lanka, and other exotic places.

At one point he dropped a pearl of a story on us. We thought he goes to these cool places, charters a boat, puts on scuba equipment, dives in, and starts looking.

Nope.

He's much more efficient than that. He goes to fishing villages and checks the catches of fishing boats. "Why should I be one guy in the water looking for sharks when I can see what fifty or sixty boats have caught?"

Dave is harnessing the power of complementary people. The probability that your knowledge, time, and energy are all that's needed is low. Steve Jobs needed Steve Wozniak at Apple. Melanie Perkins needed Cliff Obrecht and Cameron Adams at Canva. And Dave Ebert needed fishing boat captains.

Figure 5.6   Dave Ebert with the skeleton of a fourteen-foot great white shark, 2023.

(Source: Guy Kawasaki)

Whether you're hunting sharks, revolutionizing computing, or democratizing design, there are conditions that make complements, well, complementary. I learned this from *Is It Time to Consider Co-CEOs?* by Marc A. Feigen, Michael Jenkins, and Anton Warendh. They studied 87 publicly traded companies (which is late in the life cycle of organizations) to develop this list:

- Willing participants. Both people have to want to operate in this way.
- Complementary skill sets. They should have different skills, not duplicative ones.
- Clear responsibilities and decision rights. What each party does should be clear.
- Mechanisms for conflict resolution. A procedure should be in place to resolve problems.
- Appearance of unity. They need to present a united front to the organization.
- Fully shared responsibility. Both parties should be equally responsible for success or failure.
- Board support. The board of the organization must support the structure.
- Shared values. Both parties need to agree about how to treat people and the goals of the organization.
- Exit strategy. A way to unwind the structure should be in place before it's needed.

Once you find a complement, remember that their value is their different expertise, background, and ideas. Complements can enhance creativity, decision-making, problem-solving, productivity, and the workplace environment. The old adage "Two heads are better than one" is true, provided that the two heads think independently.

Identify Your Inner "Nigel"

∠ You seek methods to control your inner critic.
∠ You wish to use your inner critic to further your development.

∠ You're curious about how exceptional people handle their inner critic.

Julia Cameron, the queen of creativity and author of more than forty books including *The Artist's Way*, has an imaginary friend and inner critic named Nigel. According to Julia, he is a gay British interior designer for whom nothing she does is good enough. To quote Julia:

> *I do the morning writing every day, and Nigel says, "Oh, you're boring," and you say, "Thank you for sharing, Nigel," and you just keep on writing. What happens is that your Nigel, your critic, becomes miniaturized. It becomes a cartoon voice, and not something deadly, forbidding, looming, and frightening.*

An inner Nigel, however, is not necessarily bad—or bad all the time. It can motivate you to achieve superior results. As Gretchen Rubin, author of *Life in Five Senses*, said:

> *To be Gretchen, I must both accept myself and expect more from myself.*

It may appear trite, but naming your inner critic is beneficial because it compartmentalizes doubt into a single entity. Then the relationship can become humorous and lighthearted—and probably more constructive. So give your inner critic a name and converse with it.

Develop a Routine

∠ You seek a consistent morning ritual to save time for important decisions.

∠ You want to learn how to implement a new habit into your preexisting lifestyle.

∠ You want your routine to generate positive feelings and momentum.

Julia Cameron and many other guests on Remarkable People extolled the benefit of daily routines. The goal is to get a rolling start every day.

Figure 5.7   My daily breakfast: peanut butter and bananas on toast with coffee, 2023. I prefer Skippy Super Chunk on nine-grain bread from the Whole Grain Natural Bread Company.

(Source: Guy Kawasaki)

Rather than vacillate about what to do first, you just start every day with the same activity. Julia's routine is to write three pages of longhand text as a stream of consciousness every morning. My routine is to drink one cup of coffee and eat one piece of toast with peanut butter and a sliced banana.

The goal is to get in motion and save your brain power for important choices. So get up, write your morning journal, and get going. The world needs you to be focused—not choosing outfits to wear.

BJ Fogg, professor and founder of the Behavior Design Lab at Stanford, provided a way to make morning routines and other desirable habits easier to embrace.

> *You take whatever habit you want, whether it's meditation or doing squats or pushups, or reading, and you make it super tiny. So maybe meditation is three breaths, maybe it's two squats, maybe just reading a paragraph.*
>
> *And then you design it into your existing routine.*

And so you figure out, "What does this naturally come after? What does reading naturally come after in my existing routine? Maybe it comes after I turn off my computer for the day. That's when I read." For me, I found that pushups come naturally after I pee. So after I pee, I do two push-ups. That's the recipe.

And so, those are the two hacks. One, you make it tiny. Two, you don't use any external reminders. You use your existing routine to be your reminder. So you're finding where it fits, where it will flow. And then the third hack is how you wire it in to make it become automatic. And that's by causing yourself to feel a positive emotion.

So if you feel a positive emotion as you do a behavior, that behavior becomes more automatic. In other words, it becomes a habit. And in tiny habits, you don't leave that to chance. You hack your emotions. You deliberately feel a positive emotion, so the habit will wire in quickly.

Identify a specific, attainable routine that works for you. There is no requirement for length or detail. Beginning modestly and staying consistent are the keys to success.

Break Bad Habits

∠ You want to combine enjoyment with tasks to overcome impulsiveness.

∠ You're wondering if public commitments can help you avoid procrastination.

∠ You want to learn how to establish routines and reduce friction to help combat laziness.

Katy Milkman is a professor of operations, information, and decisions at Wharton and the next Bob Cialdini, the godfather of influence. (You'll learn more about him in the next chapter.) Her remarkable book, *How to Change: The Science of Getting from Where You Are to Where You Want to Be*, explains how to break bad habits that are preventing you from moving beyond Eureka:

■ Impulsivity. Reducing impulsivity necessitates overcoming the diversion of instant gratification by combining what you should do with what you enjoy doing—for example, exercise and movie watching. Adding gaming and competitive elements via a public leaderboard showing how much people have exercised can also help.

■ Procrastination. To decrease procrastination, it is necessary to overcome inertia. Here are some strategies: First, make a public commitment so that inaction causes embarrassment; second, use defaults so that you must opt out of an action, such as saving money, rather than opting in; and third, make a deal with yourself that if you fail, you must do something distasteful, such as, in my case, donating to the Republican National Committee.

■ Laziness. Katy offers three recommendations for combating laziness. First, establish a streak-setting objective. How many consecutive days can you write at least 1,000 words? Second, combine what you need to do with habits you already have, such as a rule prohibiting surfing until you've written 1,000 words. Third, reduce friction. For instance, I could configure my computer to automatically launch Microsoft Word upon startup, allowing me to immediately begin writing.

■ Insecurity. You can take three steps to combat a lack of confidence. First, allow yourself "exemptions" for setbacks and failures. Second, keep in mind that despite obstacles, people can change and improve. Third, become a mentor or join a support group because assisting others can facilitate your own progress.

■ Conformity. The power of conformity kicks in when you are influenced by the people around you. When you associate with successful people, you are more likely to become successful. When you associate with unsuccessful people, you are more likely to become unsuccessful. Bottom line: pick your friends carefully.

These are effective methods for breaking bad habits. They will not instantly transform you into a remarkable person, but slow and steady wins the race. If you improve just a little bit every day, you will be gratified by the end result over time,

Forget Balance, Think *Ikigai*

∠ You want to find the intersection of interest, skill, and money-making activities.

∠ You're wondering about work–life balance while trying to make a difference.

∠ You want to continue exploring interests until you discover the life purpose that motivates you.

If you want a balanced life of equal portions of work, personal, and family time, you might have to go to work for a big, successful company and hope you never get laid off. If you want to be remarkable and make a difference, you may be facing an unbalanced life and years of toil and sacrifice.

In fact, if you find your *ikigai*, you may not even ponder a "balanced life." This is a Japanese term that roughly translates to one's purpose or driving force in life. The word is made of two parts. *Iki* means life, and *gai* means worth or value.

Hector Garcia, author of *Ikigai: The Japanese Secret to a Long and Happy Life*, introduced the concept to me. In a perfect world, your *ikigai* is the intersection of what you love doing, what you're good at doing, and what you can make money doing.

However, this is not a perfect world. Therefore, I would argue that a better definition of *ikigai* is the intersection of what you love to do, what you are willing to work hard to improve, and what you don't care about getting paid to accomplish.

By my definition, writing and podcasting are my two "ikiguys," and your *ikigai* can be teaching, programming, photography, filling cavities, filmmaking, restoring furniture, removing plastic from the ocean, or crafting samurai swords.

As an example, here's how Kelly Gibson, one of my favorite guests, described her *ikigai* teaching career in Rogue River, Oregon (population 2,400):

> At the end of the day, my life's purpose has, seemingly from early on, always been, "I want to make the world a little bit better place. I want to make my students' lives work better than they would have had I not been able to be there and put time and energy into them."

Figure 5.8   Kelly Gibson working with students at Rogue River Junior/Senior High School, 2023.

(Source: Kelly Gibson)

When you talk about what you do in this kind of way, you've found your *ikigai*. I hope you find yours soon, but don't despair if you don't. It may be that instead of finding your *ikigai,* it finds you and grows over time.

Savor Your Shit Sandwich

∠ You want to find work you love even if it means enjoying "shit sandwiches" that others hate.

∠ You wonder if liking the sacrifices others typically avoid reveals your competitive advantage.

∠ You believe the emergence of your grit from shitty tasks signifies the finding of your *ikigai*.

The real-world test to determine if you have found your *ikigai* comes from Mark Manson, author of *The Subtle Art of Not Giving a F*ck: A Counterintuitive Approach to Living a Good Life*. He told me that you'll know you found your calling when you enjoy the shit sandwiches that it requires.

That is, you love to do what most people consider shit work. Writing involves the shit sandwich of rewriting and revising text over and over and over. I spend hundreds of hours doing this for each book. (The Mahalo section at the end of the book contains a list of all the locations where I worked on the book.)

Here's the Gospel of Shit Sandwich from Mark. Come to find out, we share a love of the same shit sandwich!

I kind of get a sick pleasure out of rewriting the same paragraph seven times. Most people don't, though, but that's why I'm a writer and they're not. There are other people who really, really, really enjoy spreadsheets. And that's why they're an accountant or a data analyst or whatever.

So instead of thinking about the benefits you want, think about the sacrifices that you enjoy . . . that most people don't because that's where your competitive advantage is.

I hope that one day you will ask yourself, "Why do I enjoy doing what my friends think is shit work?" Or someone asks you with admiration, "Why do you do that shit work?" That is the day that your *ikigai* has manifested itself, and I mean this in the most complimentary way: your grit has turned to shit.

Don't Argue, Just Adopt

∠ You want rules of thumb for the common daily tasks.
∠ You don't have the time or the energy to try to optimize everything you do.
∠ You like lists and straightforward instruction.

These are my tips for mastering the common tasks of a professional career. By performing these tasks well, you will be more likely to achieve success and therefore increase your self-confidence. I could explain each of the tips in detail, but if you've read this far, I'm confident you'll just believe me. ☺

Social Media

- Stay positive or stay silent.
- Assume that every post on every platform is seen by everyone.
- Don't try to change people's minds.

LinkedIn

- Complete your profile—if you're not on LinkedIn, you don't exist.
- Don't try to sell anything.
- Never disclose that you're "looking for new opportunities."

Online Conferencing

- Use an external camera and an external mic.
- Place the camera above eye level.
- Place light sources in front of you.

Email

- Write a compelling subject line, maximum five words.
- Use five or fewer sentences, in this order: what you want, who you are, why the recipient should agree, when you need it by, and what's the next step.
- Add a signature with your name, company, email address, and cell number.

Speaking

- Circulate with the crowd before you go on stage.
- Educate, don't sell.
- Use ten slides in twenty minutes with a minimum thirty-point font.

Pitching

- Explain what you do in the first two minutes.
- Incorporate a story and a demo.
- Use ten slides in twenty minutes with a minimum thirty-point font.

In-Person Meeting

- Take handwritten notes.
- Regurgitate to confirm what you heard.
- Follow up in less than thirty-six hours.

Demonstrating Your Product

- Show "how," not "what."
- Seduce, don't bludgeon.
- Reduce or eliminate dependency on Internet access.

Managing Up

- Make your boss look good.
- Make yourself indispensable.
- Bring solutions, not problems and questions.

Managing Down

- Empower people to do great work.
- Get out of their way.
- Don't ask employees to do anything that you wouldn't do.

Writing

- Write one page every day.
- Use the active voice. For example, "I caught a wave" is better than "A wave was caught by me."
- Use stories, similes, and metaphors—not adjectives and adverbs.

In this world of constant change, the ability to respond quickly and intelligently can make all the difference. Trust in the value of my experiences and allow these snippets of wisdom to guide you toward efficiency and effectiveness. Let's not argue, just adopt!

Make Decisions Right

- ∠ You angst over making perfect decisions.
- ∠ You think that decisions are the hard part and implementation is easy.
- ∠ You recognize that there's no such thing as the perfect decision.

On my birthday in August 2023, I interviewed Ellen Langer, professor of psychology at Harvard. She is the author of *The Mindful Body* and eight other books and is known as the "mother of mindfulness."

In the middle of our ninety-minute conversation, she dropped a gem that had a profound impact on my mindset:

> *The way we think we should make decisions is that you know what's going to happen, what's good or bad about different outcomes, you add them up in some complicated way, and then you do what that cost benefit analysis leads you to do. Wrong! Nobody does it. It doesn't make sense to do it . . . .*
>
> *So what's the bottom line? Since you can't make the right decision, make the decision right.*

She's saying you should make careful decisions but all the variables, anticipated and unanticipated, make "perfect" decisions an illusion. So take your best shot, focus on making your decision right, and don't look back. Remarkable people get things done. They don't just second-guess themselves.

Additional Resources

- Cameron, Julia. *The Artist's Way: A Spiritual Path to Higher Creativity.*
- Delbourg-Delphis, Maryléne. *Beyond Eureka! The Rocky Roads to Innovating.*
- Duckworth, Angela. *Grit: The Power of Passion and Perseverance.*
- Fogg, BJ. *Tiny Habits: The Small Changes That Change Everything.*
- Garcia, Hector. *Ikigai: The Japanese Secret to a Long and Happy Life.*
- Manson, Mark. *The Subtle Art of Not Giving a F*ck: A Counterintuitive Approach to Living a Good Life.*
- Milkman, Katy. *How to Change: The Science of Getting from Where You Are to Where You Want to Be.*
- O'Mara, Margaret. *The Code: Silicon Valley and the Remaking of America.*
- Rubin, Rick. *The Creative Act: A Way of Being.*
- Ueland, Brenda. *If You Want to Write: A Book about Art, Independence and Spirit.*

6

Sell Your Dream

A dream you dream alone is only a dream. A dream you dream together is reality.

— John Lennon

Get Your Foot in the Door

∠ You seek greater understanding of the sales process.
∠ You need clarity on the purpose of a sales pitch.
∠ You want advice on how to get your foot in the door.

I've endured hundreds of pitches and proposals in my time—pitches for sales, pitches for money, pitches for partnerships, and pitches for jobs. The flaw in many of them was that people think the goal of a pitch is an immediate, sale, investment, offer, or acceptance.

Wrong. Wrong. Wrong. Wrong. The purpose of most pitches is to avoid elimination and to stay in the game—which usually means continued engagement, conversation, and discussion. I have seldom seen instant acceptance and approval despite many people's efforts to achieve "shock and awe" closes.

Temple Grandin, the cattle-whisperer, visual-thinking professor from Colorado State University, recommends a "30-Second Wow

Pitch" that *shows* what you can do so that you don't need to *explain* what you can do. This means showing your portfolio of work samples, diagrams, photos, and testimonials in the same length of time as a Super Bowl commercial. The lack of a "good" educational background and work experience don't matter if you wow people in thirty seconds with proof of your competence.

This image on the next page shows an example of a Temple Grandin diagram that would wow me if I were looking for someone to help me design a ranch and would lead me to continue the discussion with the designer and let them get their foot in the door.

The same principle applies to consumer sales too. Warby Parker, purveyor of eyeglasses and contacts, enables people try on eyeglass frames in three remarkably easy ways:

- Go to its website, select frames, turn on the camera in your computer, and see the frames superimposed on your face.
- Download its smartphone app, pick frames, and see the frames superimposed on your face.
- Try five frames for five days. Warby Parker ships the frames to your house and pays postage both ways.

The purpose of a pitch is to gain access through the door and prevent it from being shut. As long as you're not locked out, you're still in the game and have a chance to compete until you are the only one left. That's called a "win" in my book.

Get Your Early Adopters

∠ You are wondering how a nutcase becomes an innovator.
∠ You want to figure out how to get more people to believe in what you're doing.
∠ You'd like to learn a conceptual framework for the propagation of new ideas.

Derek Sivers created one of the greatest marketing videos of all time in February 2010. In his TED Talk, Derek showed how a

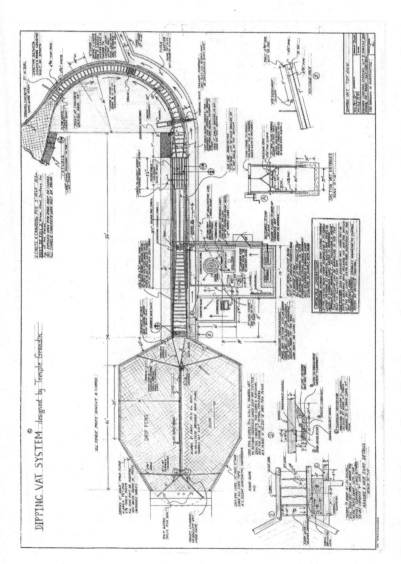

Figure 6.1 Temple Grandin's design for a tipping vat system. This is an example of a "30-Second Wow Pitch." She drew it by hand as opposed to using computer-aided design software.

Figure 6.2   Examples of Madisun and my daughter virtually trying on Warby Parker eyeglasses and letting the company "get its foot in the door"—or at least "frame on the face." Which one do you think they should order?

(Source: Madisun Nuismer and Nohemi Kawasaki)

Figure 6.3   The "dancing guy" progresses from one nutcase to a crowd.

(Source: Derek Sivers)

shirtless guy at the 2009 Sasquatch! Music Festival remarkably transforms strangers into a crowd of people dancing together.

Go to YouTube and watch "First Follower: Leadership Lessons from Dancing Guy." And then let's analyze its lessons:

- The "innovator" must be willing to look ridiculous as the first adopter.
- What the innovator is doing is ideally easy to mimic and adopt.
- The first follower transforms the innovator from a nutcase into a leader.
- The second follower transforms the innovator and first follower from two nutcases into a group.
- The group transforms the activity into a generally accepted crowd action.

There will be times that you will feel like the shirtless dancing guy, and the more innovative your idea, the more ridiculous you might feel. This is a price of being remarkable, but once you convert a few early adopters, selling your dream gets easier and easier.

Incidentally, as of 2023, more than ten million people have watched Derek's video. Here is Derek's explanation of the back story of his performance, so that you understand that behind every amazing presentation is probably someone who is scared stiff:

> *Giving that talk was terrifying for me. When I listened to the recordings, I know I sound pretty normal, but the thing is TED doesn't let you use notes, and at that first follower talk, every sentence is perfectly synced up with that video.*
>
> *So, it has to be memorized word for word. If I miss a sentence, the whole thing is thrown off. It's a three-and-a-half-minute monologue that I had to memorize word for word, which was hard enough.*
>
> *Anybody who's done a school play or something like that has done that. But then to do this at TED, not even a TEDx but the main stage TED, where there's Bill Gates. There's the Google guys. There's Bill Joy. There's, oh my God, all these brilliant people, and I have to get up and tell them something.*
>
> *I gave that talk, but to me, my biggest memory of that talk is how terrified I was, or it was not even rationally terrified, but my body was just freaking out as I'm giving that talk.*
>
> *Then I get off stage, and I had such a cool experience where Peter Gabriel rushed up to me and said, "Brilliant talk. Best thing I've seen in years. Absolutely wonderful, profound and poignant and pithy, just brilliant."*

Derek was "terrified," as are many people, when giving public speeches. However, Derek did not allow his fear to become incapacitating. He persevered and made a remarkable presentation, which is an important lesson.

Until you gain your first and second followers, you may be considered an isolated nutcase. Do whatever it takes to get them, and your credibility will subsequently increase. Typically, isolated nutcases are unremarkable and do not make the world a better place—though they certainly can make the world a worse place.

Grok the Gospel of Bob

∠ You want to learn ways to influence and persuade people.

∠ You want to learn strategies like likability, persuasion, and unity.

∠ You want to use selflessness and open-mindedness to gain favor from others.

Bob Cialdini is the godfather of influence and persuasion. He, like Brenda Ueland and Carol Dweck, was a major factor in my career. Here are my favorite Cialdini-isms that will accelerate the adoption of your ideas:

- Make people like you. How influential and persuasive do you find people who you don't like? End. Of. Discussion. Make yourself likeable if you want to sell them your dream.
- Use peers. Bob calls this "peersuasion." Peers are often a credible source of information (as opposed to influencers, who are often hired guns). For example, when your peers recommend a book, they may "persuade" you to read it.
- Pre-ciprocate. This is the concept of helping people before you want something from them. I recommend trusting in karma and helping a broad swath of people. Ideally, you would help people for the sheer pleasure of making the world a kinder, gentler place.
- Ask for reciprocity. Help for the sheer pleasure, but there is nothing wrong in asking for the return of a favor. In fact, it may be optimal because it enables people to repay favors and then feel better about asking you to do more, which in turn builds better relationships.
- Provide social proof. People want to fit into social norms. For example, when people see lots of people using a product or service, they will become interested in it. Back around 2002, when people began seeing many white iPod earbuds, resistance was futile.
- Demonstrate expertise. When Joe Roberson, my remarkable otolaryngology doctor, and Dana Suskind, director of the

University of Chicago Medicine's Pediatric Hearing Loss and Cochlear Implant program, told me that a cochlear implant would change my life, I hopped right onto the operating table because of their expertise.

- Demonstrate scarcity. When people think there's a limited quantity of something, it becomes more valuable to them. For example, there was a limited number of Gmail accounts available when Google introduced its email service. Scarcity is often bullshit—such as the limited number of copies of NFT art—but the psychological effect is real.

- Tap into commitment and consistency. People like to honor their commitments and to be consistent with what they say they're going to do. This is why organizations ask supporters to take a pledge or sign a document at the end of a recruitment drive.

- Foster unity. Most people want to be part of something and share a common identity. It can be as silly as dancers on the lawn or as important as activists in the #MeToo movement, but fostering unity is a powerful way to garner support. Much of the appeal of Macintosh user groups, for example, was hanging around people with a similar love of the world's best computer.

- Demonstrate a trend. Bob told me that people extrapolate data, so it's powerful to demonstrate a trend. A single data point isn't nearly as powerful. For example, a 10% market share may be a huge accomplishment, but it's not as powerful as saying "In year one we had 3%. In year two, it was 5%. In year three it was 10%." People will assume your market share will continue to grow.

- Promote helping others over helping oneself. Indicating that you are not seeking assistance for yourself but to help others is an effective method. For example, it's hard for people to turn down a request to help kids. They may not care about the person asking, but they do care about the kids in general.

- Use converts. Rather than trying to overwhelm people with data, it is often more effective to use converts as examples to change their minds. C. P. Ellis, a former "exalted cyclops" of the Ku Klux Klan, developed a relationship with a Black activist named Ann Atwater and had a change of heart regarding Black people as a result. This event occurred in Durham, North Carolina, in the late 1960s and was a powerful illustration of how relationships can change as people get to know each other.

Bob is to persuasion and influence as Carol Dweck is to growth mindset. I have used his principles and ideas successfully hundreds of times, and without them I would not have accomplished many of my goals, so please give his strategies a shot.

Find Something in Common

∠ You want to build connections and find common ground with others.

∠ You aim to persuade and influence others through shared interests.

∠ You seek to foster friendships, even with those who hold different views.

I once spoke to a Macintosh user group in Mobile, Alabama, and a white guy said to me, "You know Guy-ya, I was born too late for slavery and too early for robots."

I laughed when he said this, but I was thinking: "I may not be Black, but I'm not exactly white. Your people put my people in internment camps in World War II." If we didn't share a love of Macintosh, we might not have had a friendly encounter.

Making a difference and becoming remarkable necessitates building relationships and persuading people. You have a choice: you can focus on what divides you, or you can focus on what interests you share to foster a connection. With a modicum of effort, I guarantee you can find something in common with almost anyone.

Here's how:

- Start with the basics. There's always food, weather, traffic, and family. Who doesn't like BBQ, nice weather, light traffic, and kids? (Okay, BBQ might be a little risky if either of you is a vegetarian. I admit that I don't mention what great ribs I recently ate when I talk to Jane Goodall.)

- Harness the power of observation. Look at how a person dresses, what computer or phone they use, and what books they are reading. There's usually something you can observe that will provide a conversation starter.
- Do your homework. Shame on you if you don't use LinkedIn, a chatbot, a search engine, and social media platforms to learn more about a person before you meet. These tools make it trivially easy to find something you have in common with most people.

Keep your eye on the goal, which is to make your product, service, organization, or idea successful, not to create a circle of homogenous acquaintances. Focus on the big picture and learn to ignore the rest.

If you ever encounter me, feel free to ask me about BBQ, surfing, podcasting, and Macintosh. We will almost certainly end the conversation as friends. But please do not tell me that you enjoyed reading *Rich Dad, Poor Dad* or that you love my motorcycles.

Tell Good Stories

∠ You want to use storytelling to engage with others.
∠ You wish to understand how to tell good stories.
∠ You wonder about the impact of stories over facts.

David Aaker, the godfather of branding, extols the advantage of storytelling as a method to garner support. Stories are easier to tell and to remember. Plus, it's hard to dispute a story.

By contrast, there are two problems with facts. First, facts are difficult to communicate in memorable ways. Second, people can easily cite contradicting facts because few issues are truly "black and white."

Aaker provides this blueprint for good stories:

- Provide a narrative arc. Good stories are short, yet have a clear beginning, middle, and end. These qualities make good stories easier to understand and remember. It helps if your story has a surprise ending too.

- Be authentic. Good stories ring true and do not require ungodly leaps of faith. They align with your product or service and provide substance to your marketing and branding.
- Grab attention. The flow of your story must be intriguing, interesting, and fascinating. According to Aaker, "Without attention, nothing matters." I would advise avoiding "blah" adjectives such as "funny" and using similes and metaphors instead. For example, "She's witty like George Takei" is more powerful than "She's funny."
- Evoke strong emotions. What makes stories interesting and spreadable is that they generate strong emotions such as love, hope, sadness, joy, envy, and anger.
- Communicate a simple, significant lesson. Consider this Aesop's fable. A lion spares the life of a mouse. Later, the lion is ensnared in a net, and the mouse comes to his rescue by gnawing through it. Lesson: be nice to everyone because you never know who can help you in the future.

Consider the influence that stories can have. For instance, in 1975, a sixteen-year-old Nordstrom employee named Craig Trounce refunded a customer $25 because the customer was unhappy with tires he had purchased.

This story is legendary because the customer purchased the tires from the former occupant of the building. Nordstrom had taken over the location, but it did not sell him the tires. Despite this, Trounce decided to do whatever it took to make the customer happy.

This story is more compelling than any quantitative "customer satisfaction score" or marketing campaign. This illustrates how a good story is a powerful tool for remarkable people and organizations.

Open Your Architecture

∠ You want to explore how integration with other products can lead to success.

∠ You need to weigh the benefits and drawbacks of this approach.

∠ You wonder how to ultimately choose between open and closed architectures.

This is technical jargon for creating products and services that other organizations can supplement with features and functionality. This enables other organizations not only to buy into your dreams, but also to integrate their products into your dreams as well.

For example, when Sony introduced its Alpha series of mirrorless cameras, an initial weakness was the lack of different lenses. Sony did not have the resources to create both new cameras and also all the necessary lenses.

However, Sony supported the efforts of other companies to create compatible lenses, and by 2023, the availability of Sony-compatible lenses from companies such as Tamron and Sigma was a reason to buy a Sony camera and not a Canon or Nikon camera.

However, an open architecture involves extra work and a commitment to the big picture:

- Sharing the pie in the pursuit of baking a bigger pie. Sony is foregoing revenue from lens sales by allowing Tamron and Sigma to sell Sony-compatible lenses.

- Documenting how your product or service works at its root level so that others can understand it too and make compatible products.

- Providing support to external parties as they come up to speed with the technical requirements for building compatible products.

There is also an argument for a closed architecture. In this scenario, a camera manufacturer would not enable any other products to work with its camera, thus maximizing its own revenue. Controlling the system can mean better integration and a smoother customer experience.

I favor an open architecture but either method can work. And both at the same time can work too. Apple's computers, for example, are "closed" to most hardware changes, but the iOS and Macintosh app stores are "open" to application developers.

Thousands of applications created by these developers have increased the functionality of Apple's products. My experience at Apple taught me that an open architecture is an effective method for recruiting others to your team, evangelizing your vision, and achieving success.

Don't Hear "No"

∠ You want to perceive rejection as a temporary setback, not a permanent denial.

∠ You need to avoid generalizing a negative response, treating each "No" as an isolated case.

∠ You wonder how to reframe a refusal, using it as a motivation to ultimately transform it into a "Yes."

As my friend Shellye Archambeau, who wrote *Unambiguously Ambitious*, was ascending corporate America she didn't hear "No" for an answer. People may have said no, but Shellye heard them say, "Not yet" or "Not now." Maybe she even heard, "Yes, if." She certainly didn't hear, "Not now or ever and go away." This kind of grit and invulnerability to vulnerability are necessary to become remarkable and make a difference, so don't give up.

Also, don't generalize a negative response. For example, if one company doesn't offer you a job, don't conclude you're unemployable. Or if one college rejects you, this doesn't mean you won't get into any college at all.

This is especially true in venture-capital fundraising. Melanie Perkins, CEO of Canva, pitched the company to 300 venture capitalists over a three-year period before any said yes. If she had given up on raising capital after the first 299 rejections, Canva might not exist today. (See Figure 6.4.)

Don't consider "No" as a conclusion. When you hear it, take advantage of it. Consider it outside of its typical negative context, and frame it in a way that encourages you to keep trying. Do so and the "No" will hopefully transform into a "Yes."

Figure 6.4   Six of the typical rejections that Melanie Perkins received after pitching Canva. As of the fall of 2023, Canva had 165 million monthly active users.

(Source: Canva investor presentation, November 2023)

"Let a Hundred Flowers Blossom"

∠ You want to embrace being open to unintended uses of your product.

∠ You need to build on accidental successes, understanding that market forces often reposition your product.

∠ You wonder if focusing on early adopters can lead to further success.

"Let a hundred flowers blossom" is a line stolen from Chairman Mao Zedong, although I fail to see how he implemented it. My advice is to let any kind of flower blossom and be thankful that anything blossoms at all.

For example, in 1984 Apple intended Macintosh to become a spreadsheet, word processing, and database computer. Apple went zero for three as the IBM PC remained the go-to computer for these functions. Instead Aldus and Adobe, two software startups, created software that enabled people to use Macintoshes to publish books, magazines, and newspapers.

Figure 6.5 Macintosh 128K, introduced on January 24, 1984, in Cupertino, California.

(Source: Apple)

We wanted a general productivity computer, but independent software companies and our customers created a "desktop publishing" machine. Hallelujah! I learned to take the win and build upon it. Ultimately, the market—not you—is what controls the positioning of your products and services.

Just be thankful that anything isn't invasive or a fire hazard. To return to my acorns and oaks metaphor, it's as if I planted acorns but wind-dispersed coyote bush and maple seeds landed on my hill and took root. Works for me!

This chart shows more examples of seeds that blossomed in unintended ways.

Name	Intended Use	Actual Use
Viagra	Treatment of angina and high blood pressure	Treatment of erectile dysfunction
Bubble wrap	Textured wallpaper	Protective packaging
Duct tape	Waterproofing ammunition cases	Everything

The way this works is that you do your best to create a great product or service, take your best guess at positioning it, and then see what happens. Maybe you were right all the way along, but be prepared for surprises at who adopts your product or service and what they do with it.

Then "take the sale" and be thankful. Do things to increase the satisfaction of your early adopters and establish a foothold with them. Then proceed to other markets and industries.

Optimize the Day

∠ You'd like to learn how to turn negative occurrences into opportunities.
∠ You want to then make the most of opportunities.
∠ You would love to learn about a young person who is kicking butt.

Olivia Julianna is the twenty-something Gen Z political activist I mentioned in the introduction of this book. She seized a congressman's tasteless attempt to body-shame her and optimized it into a $2.5 million fundraiser for abortion rights.

Anyone who turns a congressman's tweets into $2.5 million knows how to seize and optimize the day, so I asked her for her top three tips to optimally use opportunities to effectuate change.

Here is her answer:

1. *A broad coalition is best. Whether you are somebody who is more ideologically aligned with Joe Biden, Bernie Sanders, or Stacey Abrams, at the end of the day we all agree on the core tenets. Don't alienate people because you disagree on the semantics, even though you agree on the core principles.*
2. *Be clear about what it is you want to accomplish. If I want to fundraise for abortion, then I'm going just flat out say I'm fundraising for abortion because Matt Gaetz attacked me. Every single time you have attention, that is an opportunity to catalyze change.*
3. *When you do have an action, make sure that it's something that people can do. It's easy for me to ask people to donate to abortion funds. Even if the ask is retweeting to raise awareness, always ask people for something and make the ask as easy as you possibly can.*

Figure 6.6   Olivia Julianna accepting the Marie C. Wilson Emerging Leader Award at the Ms. Foundation "Women of Vision Awards" in New York, 2023.

(Source: Kevin Mazur/Getty Images)

You can use Olivia's techniques to make a difference and to be a remarkable person. She has used this approach successfully and turned attacks into optimized opportunities to unify people, clarify purpose, and catalyze collective action.

Show up in Person

∠ You want to learn how to build trust.

∠ You need to understand the value of personal presence.

∠ You wonder if personal interactions can strengthen relationships.

One last tip about selling your dream. Lin-Manuel Miranda is an actor, playwright, singer, and composer. He created and starred in *Hamilton* and *In the Heights*. He has won three Tony Awards, three Grammy Awards, an Emmy Award, and a MacArthur Fellowship. No doubt he's remarkable.

Jon M. Chu, the director and screenwriter of *Crazy Rich Asians* and *In the Heights* (and also a remarkable person) told me this story about working with Miranda on the film version of *In the Heights*.

Figure 6.7   Jon M. Chu and Lin–Manuel Miranda about to enjoy some ice cream on the set of *In the Heights*, June 2019.

(Source: Jose Perez/Bauer-Griffin/Getty Images)

We had a meeting for extras in the neighborhood. I never go to extras gatherings.

They gather extras. They take pictures. They put them on a wall. I go there, they precut them. I go into a room full of hundreds of pictures, and I pick the type of whatever environment I want the school to be in or the environment that I want this scene to be in.

So I never go to the place where they take the picture.

He called me and asked, "Where are they doing that?" I said, "Oh, down the street at the theater." And he said, "I'm going."

He goes there and makes a speech to these people of how much this means to him, how much this means to the community, how much he appreciates them.

That's the sign of a true leader. Took time out of Lin-Manuel Miranda's day, which is a packed, full day . . . he doesn't have time for anything. He'll make it for his neighborhood.

Never underestimate the power of showing up in person. Lin-Manuel Miranda's presence at the extras casting, despite his packed schedule, demonstrated respect for his community and appreciation for their involvement. And Jon M. Chu's bringing it up in our interview shows Jon's awareness of the importance of showing up in person.

Lin-Manuel was aware that his personal interactions would have an impact, and they did. Your presence communicates that you care and are invested in the process, thereby strengthening relationships and establishing trust.

Become a Mission-Driven Asshole

∠ You want to understand what made Steve Jobs a remarkable leader and CEO.

∠ You need to understand different leadership types and if one is optimal.

∠ You wish to develop a relationship with others in which critique is viewed as a positive.

Do I need to tell you any more about Tony Fadell than that he created the iPod, iPhone, and Nest thermostat? These inventions are three of *Time's* "50 Most Influential Gadgets of All Time." If you had created one, you'd be doing great. If you created three, that's a trend, and you're remarkable.

In 2022 Tony published a book called *BUILD: An Unorthodox Guide to Making Things Worth Making*, in which he makes the case for mission-driven asshole CEOs. According to Tony, there are four kinds of assholes:

- Political. These people are concerned with surviving and making themselves look good by sucking up. They also work behind the scenes to undermine others.
- Controlling. These are the micromanagers who are threatened by talented people. No one else has good ideas except them, and they seek to control even the minutiae of the workplace.
- Ego-driven. This is the purest form of asshole: mean, crude, manipulative, defensive, and angry. You would cross the street to avoid saying hello to them.
- Mission-driven. Steve Jobs embodies this type. Dedicated to the mission of the organization, they steamroll people who aren't excellent. They care a lot. They work hard. They listen and change their minds if you are right.

This is what Tony told me about working for Steve and what it means to be a mission-driven asshole:

He wasn't an ego-driven asshole, not at least from what I can see. He cared that the mission was right and right on.

You don't judge the people. You judge and critique the work that those people do. You make sure that you're doing it in support of what's going to be the best for the customer and educating.

But you're going to be relentless. You're going to make sure that the team just doesn't take second best. They go find the best. Literally drive every single one of the details that matter.

I wish that leading an organization is always unicorns farting pixie dust while singing "Kumbaya," but this isn't true. There will be times that you have to practice tough love and push your team members.

For example, they may do mediocre work, and you need to make them redo it, perhaps more than once until you determine that it cannot be improved. They may believe that you are an asshole or at least possess asshole traits.

It's worse if your team thinks you're a pushover who doesn't demand excellent performance. What matters is why you are acting like an asshole. Is it for your own ego? To cover your insecurities? Or because you want them to do the best work of their career and succeed?

For the record, I don't know anyone from the Macintosh Division who didn't think Steve Jobs was an asshole. But I don't know anyone from the Macintosh Division who didn't think it was an honor and privilege to work for him, and I'm sure we would all do it again if we had the chance.

Focus on What's Important

∠ You want to recognize personal expression in choices like clothing and hairstyle.

∠ You need to understand how societal biases influence these choices.

∠ You wonder about the strategic impact of not conforming to expectations.

Figure 6.8   Michelle Obama at the 2016 Democratic National Convention.

(Source: Alex Wong/Getty Images)

In 2020 I got into a discussion about the hairstyles of Black women with Julie Lythcott-Haims, who is an author, speaker, Palo Alto City Council member, and former dean at Stanford. Her conclusion: "It's on us as Black women to wear the hair that makes us feel beautiful and proud."

However, Michelle Obama had spoken with pressed hair at the 2016 Democratic National Convention, so I asked Julie what to make of that. My thinking was that of all Black women in the world, Michelle Obama could wear her hair "natural" or any other way she wanted.

Here's Julie's response:

> There are a lot of folks still even in her intended audience, the Democratic Party, who would see a Black woman wearing her hair natural as being inappropriate. They would see it as less professional and not what it, quote unquote, "should" be. I think Michelle Obama knows that.
>
> So when she is asked to ascend to an important podium and give one of the greatest speeches of her life, she's probably being very strategic and thinking, "Today is a day for pressed hair because that will be what will allow me to be heard by the most people."

There's no doubt that complex and nuanced conversations about issues such as Black women's hair reveal important societal expectations and biases. However, weigh these issues against the message that you wish to convey and the impact you seek.

Additional Resources

- Aaker, David. *Aaker on Branding: 20 Principles That Drive Success.*
- Archambeau, Shellye. *Unapologetically Ambitious: Take Risks, Break Barriers, and Create Success on Your Own Terms.*
- Berger, Jonah. *The Catalyst: How to Change Anyone's Mind.*
- Berger, Jonah. *Contagious: Why Things Catch On.*
- Berger, Jonah. *Invisible Influence: The Hidden Forces That Shape Behavior.*
- Cialdini, Bob. *Influence: The Psychology of Persuasion.*

- Cialdini, Bob. *Pre-Suasion: A Revolutionary Way to Influence and Persuade.*
- Lythcott-Haims, Julie. *How to Raise an Adult: Break Free of the Overparenting Trap and Prepare Your Kid for Success.*
- Lythcott-Haims, Julie. *Your Turn: How to Be an Adult.*
- Milkman, Katy. *How to Change: The Science of Getting from Where You Are to Where You Want to Be.*

STAGE 3

Grace—Uplift and Inspire

7 | Lead by Example

Graceful leadership is about leading by example and showing others how to live with kindness, compassion, and empathy.

—Dalai Lama

Embrace Grace

∠ You wish to understand the importance of grace in becoming remarkable.

∠ You want to determine the qualities that embody grace.

∠ You ponder how leadership can manifest through such grace.

Grace is the final stage of becoming remarkable. It refers to the poise, kindness, and thoughtfulness that serves to uplift and inspire others.

I observed grace in many of the remarkable people who I interviewed. The standouts include Jane Goodall, Ken Robinson, Carol Dweck, and Bob Cialdini. There is a quiet confidence about them, and their focus is not on themselves but on others and society as a whole.

Because of their grace, they set examples and lead the way for people around them, so we begin with leadership.

Get Over Imposter Syndrome

∠ You want to overcome imposter syndrome.

∠ You need to understand that this syndrome can be a humbling experience, and also a hindrance if not controlled.

∠ You wonder how to acknowledge imposter syndrome and use it to your advantage.

Over and over, female guests discussed imposter syndrome. (I cannot recall a male guest ever bringing this up, but I doubt that men don't have the same feelings.) Imposter syndrome involves feelings of inadequacy and doubt, culminating in a fear of exposure as a fraud—basically that you are not as good as people think you are.

> I have written eleven books, but each time I think, "Uh-oh, they're going to find out now. I've run a game on everybody, and they're going to find me out."
>
> —*Maya Angelou*

It's hard to be gracious if you're feeling like an imposter, so let's address this.

Viewed positively, imposter syndrome can mean that you have a sense of humility and self-awareness. This is good because it can motivate you to work harder to fulfill and exceed your lofty image. And it's better to have imposter syndrome than the narcissistic "I am awesome, and the universe owes me accolades" syndrome.

The difference between these two syndromes is "reality"—that is, are you truly as good as people think you are? If you are, then overcoming imposter syndrome is an extension of giving yourself a break. In this case, you need to give yourself credit.

When you are racked by imposter syndrome and don't exude confidence, you can impede your own progress, so here's what to do:

- Admit that you're feeling inadequate. Put the label on it— "imposter syndrome"—so you remember that it happens so often, it's been named. Make it smaller and control it. Don't deny it.

- Assure yourself that even remarkable people sometimes feel like imposters. I would make the case that people who never feel like imposters are delusional.
- Focus on your accomplishments, growth, and doing more great stuff, so that your reality matches or exceeds your reputation. You're not an imposter if you're not an imposter.
- Seek the assurance and feedback of friends and colleagues whom you respect and trust who would also provide "tough love." When you meet or exceed their expectations, you'll know you're not an imposter.
- Fake it until you make it. The façade of confidence and optimism will help you succeed, and when you succeed, you will become confident and optimistic. Almost everyone who is remarkable goes through this progression.
- Focus on the mission or cause. When your head is spinning because of doubt and insecurity, just remember what your difference-making goal is. Everything else is noise.

"Faking it until you make it" means acting confident and secure despite your fears and doubts. This is not the same as falsifying your accomplishments or results. The actions of Elizabeth Holmes, imprisoned CEO of Theranos, were immoral and unethical, so do not confuse putting on a brave and confident face with lying.

Overcoming imposter syndrome is crucial for personal development and achievement. Remember that even the most extraordinary individuals experience these emotions. The keys to remarkableness are producing results and overcoming the feeling of being unworthy. My advice is to "wear a mask until it becomes your face."

Craft a "Good Situation"

- ∠ You want to lead effectively by creating a supportive work environment.
- ∠ You need to foster growth, cooperation, and inclusivity, such as supporting an LGBTQ+ community.

∠ You wonder how to enhance productivity and well-being by embracing principles that enable success.

The career paths of remarkable people often requires leading people. They know how to inspire and motivate others. This requires crafting a "good situation" for their colleagues and employees.

Geoffrey Cohen, professor of psychology at Stanford, evangelist of wise interventions, and author of *Belonging: The Science of Creating Connection and Bridging Divides*, developed the concept of "good situations" to enable people to do their best work.

A work environment that is a good situation embodies these qualities:

- Opportunities for growth and learning to provide motivation
- Cooperation and cohesion to increase positive interaction
- Bountiful feedback and recognition to enhance morale and efficacy

Your role is to ensure that these qualities exist in your workplace. These are your action items:

- Communicate the vision of what you want to achieve.
- Align your team to that vision and inspire them to achieve it.
- Establish high standards and expectations for everyone— including yourself.
- Provide adequate resources. "More with less" is easy for management to say. How about "more with more" instead?
- Get out of their way and "macro manage" them instead.

For example, let's craft a good situation for members of the LGBTQ+ community in a company's workforce. This would involve actions such as:

- Corporate-wide adoption of trans-inclusive policies and procedures. This includes dress codes, pronoun usage, and restroom access.

- Support for gender transition procedures such as medical procedures, counseling, and other health-care resources.
- Diversity training for employees. The goal is to provide a safe and supportive environment for LGBTQ+ people.
- Advocacy for the rights and accomplishments of LGBTQ+ people throughout society, not only within the organization.
- Heightened visibility and acceptance of LGBTQ+ employees by providing examples of success and role models within the organization.

Situation crafting in these ways can increase the productivity and well-being of the entire organization as well as the LGBTQ+ community. A good situation benefits everyone.

In essence, a remarkable leader enables the success of others; fosters their development by rewarding their commitment, perseverance, and achievements; and ultimately guides people to realize their full potential.

By the way, read the *Harvard Business Review* article "Creating a Trans-Inclusive Workplace" for more information on this particular subject.

Hire Better Than Yourself

∠ You need to recognize the value of hiring people better than yourself.

∠ You want to build a top-performing team by hiring individuals of superior quality.

∠ You wonder how to approach hiring with humility and self-confidence.

The Macintosh Division had a rule: you only hire A players—that is, people who were as good as or better than "the rest of us." (That's evidence of arrogance for sure.)

Our thinking was that A players hire A players, or even better, A+ players. This prevents sliding down the slippery slope to bozosity. By contrast, B players hire C players. C players hire D players, and so on. This is because they want to feel superior to people who work for them.

Figure 7.1   Macintosh Division in 1984. I'm in the upper left corner to the left of the guy with the glasses.

(Source: Apple)

The benefits of hiring better than yourself include:

- Expansion of knowledge and skills. Better people bring with them increased knowledge and skills that the team doesn't already possess.
- Enhanced decision-making. A good assumption is that with more knowledge and skills, your decision-making process and outcomes will improve.
- Deeper and better team. Let's face it: employees will turn over and leave. It's good to have highly qualified people to step into the vacancies.
- High-performance culture. You want people to look around the room and realize they need to be at the top of their game. This means that "excellence is expected" and "good enough isn't good enough."

Figure 7.2 Reunion of the Macintosh Division in 2019 at the home of Alain Rossman and Joanna Hoffman. It took twenty-five years, but I learned to stand in the front for photos.

The hard part about this recommendation is that it requires humility and self-confidence—the former because you have to be able to admit people are better than you, and the latter because you have to not be threatened by them.

There is no better testament to your leadership than the team you create. When you hire people, you should never settle for mediocrity. Put aside your ego and look for people who will make the organization even better, with or without you.

Negotiate Like a Champ

∠ You want to become a remarkable negotiator.
∠ You want to learn practical and tactical negotiation tips.
∠ You wonder how your negotiation tactics reflect on you.

Remarkable people are good negotiators. They get what they want and want what they get. And the people who they negotiated with want to do business again.

Please set aside notions that negotiating is about the exercise of raw power. This is only true on Netflix and Apple TV. Barry Nalebuff, professor at the Yale School of Management and author of *Split the Pie: A Radical New Way to Negotiate*, explains how to conduct win-win, gracious negotiating.

Here are his power tips to enable you to be a remarkable negotiator:

- Give the other side what it wants. Barry learned this from Cade Massey, practice professor at Wharton's Operations, Information and Decisions Department. If you start negotiation by giving the other side what it wants, you can set the expectation that you should also get what you want. "I'll buy you a new surfboard if you plant 100 oak trees on that denuded hill."

- Write the other side's press release or victory speech. Barry credits William Ury, the co-author of *Getting to Yes*, for this. This concept is to imagine what the other side would like to say in a speech or press release after negotiating with you. Then you give them that, so that you can get what you want.

- Make the other side's case. Try to make the other side's case to show that you understand their perspective. Think of this as empathetic negotiation. This can reduce argumentation and allow you to validate your side too. A greater understanding of why a party is negotiating will make you a better negotiator.

- Hardly ever say no. The word "no" is a showstopper. It signals that one side must completely concede, which just makes negotiation harder. It's better to say, "Yes, if . . ." because it presents a path to a decision. My theory is that as soon as the other side hears "yes," it thinks it got what it wants. Then it doesn't want to give up what is has and will be more willing to do what you want it to do.

- Fight fire with water. Fighting fire with fire is a technique to slow or stop a fire by reducing the supply of flammable material with a controlled burn. In human relations, however, the practice is more likely to exacerbate problems than solve them. So put out the fire and move on to something more likely to be constructive and mutually beneficial.

- Don't anchor. The concept of anchoring is to make an extreme offer to lock the other party in the range of what you want. This entails two potential problems. First, the other party may simply walk away. Second, if your next move is to make a large concession, the other party may think you will back down on other issues too. If you're going to anchor a price, ensure that it's "within reason."

The ability to negotiate successfully is essential for developing confidence. By understanding the perspective of the other party, avoiding confrontation, and employing effective strategies, you can negotiate like a pro and achieve mutually beneficial outcomes.

Put Skills First

∠ You want to know if companies are hiring candidates without formal education and degrees.

∠ You wonder what qualities companies are looking for.

∠ You wonder if you should hire people without formal education and degrees.

In the quest to hire better than yourself, the most important quality is the skills people bring to a job. There are multiple paths to achieve these skills, including formal education, work experience, and training. However, people seem to focus on "formal" education.

Temple Grandin, the cow-whispering professor, begs to differ when it comes to standardized testing and prerequisites. In particular, there are the requirements to do well in algebra and score high on standardized math tests in order to get into college:

I'm talking to students all the time trying to, let's say at community college, get a veterinary nurse degree and they're on their second and third algebra class, they're flunking, and you don't need that to be a veterinary nurse or a veterinarian.

You need arithmetic, yes, and there's a few algebraic equations for drug dosing that can be memorized. Those have to be learned, but we're screening out somebody that might be the very best veterinary nurse, actually the very best veterinarian that can visualize things wrong with animals.

While there are diagnosis, anesthetics, and dosage calculations, advanced math is probably not required by most veterinarians. Would you prefer an advanced mathematician or someone who understands animals to treat your pet? Does a divorce lawyer need to know more math than dividing by two?

When you start building a team, make the skill set of candidates your top priority—not degrees. Ginni Rometty, the first female CEO of IBM, has embraced this concept because she saw that many positions at IBM required a college degree even though the actual work didn't.

This is her epiphany about hiring non-degreed people:

We do a lot of data gathering over the years and we find that after about a year, they show the same performance as our college grads. They're taking more courses because they're thirsty. They want to keep learning. More loyal, more retentive.

Eventually it took me down a decade of work where we would relook at every job credential, and we find that 50% of our jobs did not need to start with a college degree.

Remember: this is coming from the former CEO of a company with 350,000 employees, universal brand awareness, and unlimited resources! If she can look beyond degrees, you can too.

Finding the necessary skill sets for your organization is the top priority. These skill sets may come in people who don't have college degrees, and that's okay. When you are listening, attitude and competence speak louder than degrees.

Send the Right Signals

∠ You want to create effective incentives that align with the goals of your organization.

∠ You need to consider both intended and unintended consequences of the incentive plans.

∠ You wonder how to avoid unwanted outcomes of incentives.

If you ran a taxicab company and paid your drivers by the hour, you might not be sending the right signal to them. Since it doesn't matter how many fares your drivers get if they are paid a flat rate, they may take frequent breaks and use less expedient paths to destinations.

Now, suppose you're on the board of directors of a company, and you tell the CEO that her goal is the long-term growth of shareholder value. However, her bonus is based on annual profits. Since she doesn't know how long you'll keep her around, she may try to maximize annual bonuses and avoid risky innovation that will take more than a year to complete.

Uri Gneezy is a professor of behavioral economic and strategic management at the University of California, San Diego's Rady School of Management. He is also the author of *Mixed Signals: How Incentives Really Work*. His idea is that incentives send signals, so you need to ensure that the signals are aligned with your goals.

This sounds like a "duhism" except that leaders often send confusing or contradictory signals to their organization. This isn't to say that people are pigeons tapping on levers in a lab, but he advises the following steps:

- Align incentives with the goals of the organization. This may yield another benefit: formalizing your goals, which many organizations neglect doing.
- Consider the unintended consequences of incentive plans. It's helpful to have the "fresh eyes" of your spouse or friend to review your incentive plans.
- Test and iterate as your plans roll out into the real world. Try a small sample before you implement a plan across the board.
- Incorporate "soft compensation" such as growth, recognition, and purpose into the total package.

Here is an illustration of how the best-laid incentive plans can go awry. It's from an article called "The Great Hanoi Rat Hunt: A

Conversation with Michael G. Vann." Vietnamese officials in Hanoi paid a bounty for rat tails because of an infestation of the pests.

Citizens turned in hundreds of thousands of tails for bounties, but the program was *curtailed* when officials discovered people were breeding rats, cutting off their tails, and then releasing them to foster more breeding. People even collected rats from outside Hanoi.

Can you fault them? The incentive was to turn in as many tails as you could. Better ways include an educational program about the diseases rats transmit, free resources such as poison and traps, and public certification of rat-free buildings.

Bob Cialdini, godfather of influence, might advocate social pressure: "Our neighbor's house has a sign that it is rat-free. We need to keep up with them and not endanger our neighborhood too."

The message is to ensure that your incentives and objectives are aligned. You should avoid encouraging people to take the wrong actions to achieve their objectives if you want all of you to achieve remarkable results.

Draw Boundaries

∠ You want to learn how to determine which activities to reduce and which to increase.

∠ You need help to establish clear limits on your time and communicate them.

∠ You need to practice saying no more often.

An essential skill for anyone who wants to be remarkable is drawing boundaries around demands of their time, attention, and energy. This includes both the demands they put on themselves as well as those put on them by others. Drawing boundaries yields these benefits:

- Increases time and energy to do important things
- Promotes your emotional and physical well-being
- Encourages others to enhance their capabilities to perform delegated tasks

- Fosters more meaningful (and fewer) personal and professional relationships
- Sets an example for others to also draw boundaries

Here are the steps to draw your boundaries:

- Assess where you are. How frazzled, impinged, and infringed do you feel? What are you not able to do that you want or need to do? Step one is to assess the magnitude of the problem.
- Identify and rank your priorities. Categorize your activities and relationships from the most important to the least important. This will help you clarify your priorities.
- Assess your capacity and capability. Compare your priorities with your capacity and capability. The math may jump out at you: there aren't enough hours in the day to do everything on your list.
- Define the limits. Establish measurable limits such as how much time you'll spend answering email, reading social media sites, hanging out with the gang, and working at night and on weekends.
- Communicate the limits. Explain these boundaries and limits to those around you. You may even have to communicate them to your inner compulsive yourself as well as others.
- Adapt and revise. You're unlikely to set optimum boundaries at the start, and priorities and conditions change. Don't hesitate to change your boundaries over time.

These are high-level, what-you'd-expect-to-read-online steps to draw your boundaries. Let me provide more tactical ones that I learned through personal experience and my podcast guests:

- Ask yourself this question: "At the end of my life, am I going to wish I did more _____ or more _____?" For example, will you wish you surfed more with your kids or attended more fifty-person, cameras-on-optional Zoom meetings?

- Zoe Chance, assistant professor at the Yale School of Management, recommends that you try saying no to every request for twenty-four hours. Experiencing how hard it is to do this will show you if you are too much of a "giver." Also, you'll probably see how little bad comes from saying no to people.
- Catherine Price, author of *How to Break Up with Your Phone*, suggests that you start taking back your life by avoiding checking your phone immediately before going to bed and immediately after you wake up. She predicts you will reap huge benefits from protecting these two times of day, which will encourage you to embrace even more boundaries.
- At first saying no may be difficult, and it will take getting used to. The sooner you start, the easier it will be. Just remember that saying no provides the opportunity to say yes to important things that can accelerate your success.
- Harness the power of the word "because." Harvard professor Ellen Langer found that people were more likely to comply with a request to use the photocopy machine if one used the word "because" followed by a reason—even something as weak as "because I have to make some copies."

Drawing boundaries is an important skill for becoming remarkable. By assessing one's priorities, defining limits, and communicating these limits effectively, you can efficiently manage your time, foster meaningful relationships, and promote your emotional and physical health.

Manage by Zooming Around (MBZA)

∠ You want to make relationship building a priority.
∠ You want to figure out digital ways to "walk around" and connect with people.
∠ You wonder if a return to the office is necessary.

Tom Peters, the mastermind of management excellence who wrote *In Search of Excellence*, popularized the concept of MBWA—management by walking around. This technique, similar to Toyota's *genchi genbutsu* (go and see), involves managers walking around the organization and interacting with employees in their workspace.

The goal is to increase communication, collaboration, and trust in an organization—instead of the psychological and physical separation of management and workers. The COVID-19 pandemic forced Tom to change his game and manage by Zooming around:

> *Zoom is not unemotional. Zoom is not inhumane. Yes, it's different, but I really believe that. All the things we're saying about Zoom, they said about long-distance phone calls.*
>
> *And it is just the depersonalization . . . we've been virtualizing since at least the telegraph. The telegraph was Zoom, wasn't it? Pure, raw, unmitigated Zoom. And then the telephone.*

In his book *Tom Peters' Compact Guide to Excellence*, he hammers home the point:

> *The big point here is that the MBWA concept is more important than ever— and with remote work increasingly the norm, some new form(s) of up-close-and-personal interaction must become a centerpiece of your daily activities.*

Do not underestimate the power that relationships and connections possess. It is crucial for your success in all aspects of life that you interact with others frequently. In-person interaction and communication is preferable, so opt for it whenever possible.

Shut the F★ Up

- ∠ You want to learn how to be more effective in your communication.
- ∠ You wonder how to control your emotions in difficult conversations.
- ∠ You are interested in the power of silence.

One of the ways to lead the way in a graceful manner is to listen more than you talk. I learned this from one of the funniest people I know, Dan Lyons. His blog, *The Diary of Fake Steve Jobs*, and his first

Figure 7.3   A scene from the "Exit Event" episode of *Silicon Valley*. 2019.

(Source: John Altschuler, Mike Judge, and Dave Krinsky)

two books, *Disrupted* and *Lab Rats*, lay bare the absurdities of the tech industry.

In 2023 Dan published *STFU: The Power of Keeping Your Mouth Shut in an Endlessly Noisy World*. In it he confesses that he has the fundamental flaw that he cannot shut up. This has had a negative impact on his personal and professional life—for example, HubSpot fired him because he was too outspoken, and that cost him $8 million.

And $8 million here, $8 million there . . . pretty soon it adds up to real money.

Circa 2023, "talk less, get more" is Dan's mantra, and even as a podcaster, I agree. (I like my guests to have 90% of the airtime.) Here are Dan's five ways to STFU:

- Say less or even nothing. Dan advises people to "pretend words are money and spend them wisely"—as opposed to spraying and praying and trying to be the center of attention.

- Master the power of the pause. The clerks of Ruth Bader Ginsburg learned to count, "One Mississippi . . . two Mississippi" after saying something to her before continuing on.
- Cool it on social media. If you're active on social media, consider reading more and posting less. Can you think of anyone who you wish was more active on social media?
- Learn how to listen. Many people are not listening when they are not talking. They are biding their time until they can speak. Instead of thinking about what you're going to say, think about what the other person is saying.
- Seek out silence. If all else fails, then get away, turn off, and tune out. Your fears of missing out are probably unwarranted.

Silence shows power. It means that you're in control of the pace, and you are giving people the chance to absorb what has been said. It also shows you can manage your emotions, and you take the time to understand the situation. Silence is often more eloquent than words.

Reduce Risk

∠ You want to reduce risk and increase confidence in your organization.

∠ You wonder how to improve your decision-making process.

∠ You want to be more prepared for unexpected events.

You may wonder what risk reduction has to do with confidence and grace. The link is that when you are not dealing with constant crises, you become a more self-assured and inspiring leader . . . which sets the tone for the entire organization.

General Stanley McChrystal is a retired four-star army general who served for thirty-four years. Among other tours of duty, he commanded the international security forces in Afghanistan from 2009 to 2010 and special operations forces from 2003 to 2008. In other words, he dealt with a remarkable amount of risk.

Figure 7.4   Stanley McChrystal inspects the troops during his retirement ceremony at Fort McNair in Washington, D.C., 2010.

(Source: The Washington Post / Getty Images)

McChrystal's book *Risk: A User's Guide* is the most enlightening book about leadership that I have read in the last forty years. Here's what he taught me about reducing risk:

- Test, test, test! Don't assume systems, people, and equipment will work as planned. Metaphorically or literally, cut the power and see what happens. Simulate attacks and retain devil's advocates to poke holes in what you're doing.
- Conduct premortems. Assume that you failed. Compile all the reasons why the failure occurred. Then eliminate as many of the vulnerabilities as possible. This process identifies more risks and threats because the goal is to come up with every possible threat in advance.
- Hold after-action reviews. These are assessments of what happened after an event. The goal is to document exactly what

occurred and to isolate what could or should be done differently the next time.

Risks and threats are ever-present and unavoidable. Your mission is to reduce unnecessary risk as much as you can and to increase the resiliency and capability of your team. This will result in a more-likely-to-survive organization and a confidence-inspiring environment that empowers people to make a difference.

Say "I Don't Know"

∠ You want to be a more credible and trustworthy leader.
∠ You wonder how to inspire others to learn and grow.
∠ You need to set a good example for open, honest, and transparent communication.

Take a moment and ponder what it takes for most leaders to say, "I don't know." They are the most powerful words in most conversations, but how often do you ever hear them?

Here are examples to prove it can happen:

The more I learn, the more I realize how much I don't know.

—Albert Einstein

The greatest obstacle to discovery is not ignorance—it is the illusion of knowledge.

—Daniel Boorstin

I don't know everything, but I know that if you want to succeed, you have to be willing to take risks

—Ginni Rometty

Remarkable people say "I don't know" because they know the benefits of using this powerful phrase:

■ **Credibility.** Acknowledging what you don't know adds credence to what you say you do know.

- Humility. It shows that you have a sense of humility and that you are open to listen and learn.
- Motivation. By forcing others to figure out things for themselves, you motivate them to learn how to learn.
- Transparency. You set a good example for being open, honest, and transparent. This sets the tone for the entire organization.

There are two special cases to consider when you use this phrase. First, at the start of your career or tenure in a job, when you say, "I don't know," you must continue with, "But I will find out and get the answer to you." Your job is to find solutions.

Second, if you're a manager or leader, when people ask, "What's going to happen?" or "What are we going to do?" the answer "I don't know" isn't enough. Instead, your answer must encompass hope and optimism too.

In these cases, "I don't know" is only the start of a good answer. Continue by saying, "But we are going to figure things out, work together, and give it our best efforts to succeed."

It's okay to acknowledge your own ignorance. In fact, it can increase your credibility and trustworthiness. However, be sure to express it in a way that inspires optimism.

Additional Resources

- Archambeau, Shellye. *Unapologetically Ambitious: Take Risks, Break Barriers, and Create Success on Your Own Terms.*
- Bryar, Colin. *Working Backwards: Insights, Stories, and Secrets from Inside Amazon.*
- Cohen, Geoffrey. *Belonging: The Science of Creating Connection and Bridging Divides.*
- Fadell, Tony. *Build: An Unorthodox Guide to Making Things Worth Making.*
- McChrystal, Stanley. *Risk: A User's Guide.*
- Nalebuff, Barry. *Split the Pie: A Radical New Way to Negotiate.*
- Niño, Martha. *The Other Side: From a Shack to Silicon Valley.*

- Peters, Tom. *In Search of Excellence: Lessons from America's Best Run Companies*.
- Rometty, Ginni. *Good Power: Leading Positive Change in Our Lives, Work, and World*.
- Thoroughgood, Christian, Katina Sawyer, and Jennica Webster. "Creating a Trans-Inclusive Workplace." *Harvard Business Review*, March–April 2020.
- Zimbardo, Phil. *The Lucifer Effect: Understanding How Good People Turn Evil*.

8

Take the High Road

The best way to find yourself is to lose yourself in the service of others.

—Mahatma Gandhi

Value All People

∠ You're wondering whom to believe, trust, and admire.
∠ You want to learn how to honor people who have helped you.
∠ You are looking for real-world examples of grace (as opposed to cage fights, yachts, and buyouts).

Here's a Carol Dweck story that you've never heard. It isn't about the growth mindset per se, but it demonstrates how gracious and thoughtful she is, which should make it easier to embrace her ideas. She is remarkable in every way.

During the period 2010–2019, she and I traveled around the world to deliver speeches. I gave fifty to seventy-five per year. She may have given more. When people asked me where I wrote during those years, my answer was "United Club."

151

We both lived thirty miles from San Francisco International Airport, and we happened to use the same limousine service run by a nice guy named Chris Webster. He was a one-man show—no website, no fleet of Mercedes S-Classes, just Chris and one old Lincoln Town Car.

He drove rich and famous Silicon Valley entrepreneurs, executives, and venture capitalists as they strove to achieve worldwide domination. (If you want to learn more about these moguls, check out Chris's book, *Confessions of a Chauffeur*.)

Alas, Chris died in 2019, and on Sunday, April 7, 2019, there was a memorial service for him at the Unity Palo Alto church. I attended the service with my son, Nate. It was a small affair of fifty people—no Bono or Norah Jones or Al Gore, just friends and family.

But Carol Dweck was there with her husband.

Which is to say that of the hundreds of people Chris had picked up at 5:00 a.m., waited for after midnight, and drove on holidays and

Figure 8.1   Guy, Carol Dweck, and Nate Kawasaki at the memorial services of Chris Webster, 2019.

(Source: David Goldman)

weekends for years, only Carol Dweck was there. I was already in love with her work, but when I saw her at Chris's funeral, she ascended to the top of people I admire.

She wanted to honor Chris and did not view him as merely "a driver" in her address book. She truly is a gracious person, and I hope this story will help you embrace her gospel of the growth mindset. You can tell a lot about a person by what they do when there's no money or glory involved.

Count Your Blessings

∠ You want to be more grateful.
∠ You wonder how to focus on the positive in your life.
∠ You are struggling with challenges and want to find hope.

I was not born into wealth and power, and that may have been my good fortune because a lifetime of wealth and power can lead to misery, mediocrity, and mundanity.

But I am lucky because my parents made sacrifices so that I could have a good life. They provided me with love and support plus a remarkable education, including Iolani School in Hawaii, Stanford, and UCLA.

I am lucky because my health is good. At sixty-nine I can still surf every day, and though I sometimes get migraine headaches and I am almost deaf, these are not overwhelming challenges.

I am lucky because I have a loving wife, four loving kids, and many loving friends. They are the blessings that are the most important component of my lucky life.

I am lucky because the work, writing, recording, investing, and advising that I have done have provided financial security. I lack for nothing and don't envy anyone except surfers who can hang ten on a wave.

Take a break from reading at this point and write down three of your blessings.

1.
2.
3.

Everyone I interviewed for *Remarkable People* counted their blessings even when their blessings were few and their difficulties were numerous. Everyone.

Fulfill Your Success *Oblige*

∠ You want to make a difference in the world by supporting others.

∠ You wonder how to use your success and experience to help others.

∠ You are looking for ways to give back to your community.

Jacob Martinez is the director of Digital NEST, an organization that helps Hispanic youth in Watsonville, California, develop alternate career paths to working in agricultural fields. In mid-2023 he texted me to tell me he had some good news.

Indeed he did. Yield Giving was about to support Digital NEST by donating several million dollars to the organization. Wow! Yield

Figure 8.2   Jacob Martinez at Digital NEST in Watsonville, California, 2023. The students are learning how to edit videos.

(Source: Guy Kawasaki)

Giving is the foundation set up by MacKenzie Scott, the ex-wife of Amazon founder Jeff Bezos, worth tens of billions. (She would have gotten more if John Conway was her lawyer.).

This is how the text conversation went between Jacob and me:

> *Guy: Wow. Those books and DVDs sure added up! Was it a nightmare to get through her screening?*
>
> *Jacob: We didn't even apply. Her team said they have been following our work and that she was really impressed. We did a short interview and then got a call a few months later.*

In addition to not having to apply, there are no reporting requirements and rules attached to the grant. MacKenzie is saying, "We like what you're doing. We trust you. Go do it." This is a remarkable example of gracious giving.

Fast-backward four decades to when I was in college. My father explained the concept of *noblesse oblige* to me: the idea that privilege comes with responsibility and obligation. I don't like the "*noblesse*" part because it makes the concept sound like it only applies to "royalty."

A better term is "success *oblige*"—meaning that anyone and everyone who is successful has moral responsibilities and obligations. MacKenzie Scott is a great example. However, you don't have to be a billionaire to do this.

Here are tangible ways to fulfill your success *oblige* by supporting others:

1. Mentor them.
2. Give them money.
3. Give them your products or services.
4. Buy their products or services.
5. Promote and recommend their products or services.
6. Jointly develop products, services, or programs.
7. Act as a reference.
8. Set a good example.

These eight activities should keep you busy for quite some time, if not for the rest of your life. By performing them, you will make a difference, even if only for a few individuals.

Help Others Succeed

∠ You wonder how to optimize your volunteer efforts.

∠ You need some specific ideas for how to help others.

∠ You want to learn more about the concept of "helper's high."

The gracious act of fulfilling your success *oblige* by helping others is a component of being remarkable, so let's spend some time optimizing the process.

Allan Luks is the co-author of *The Healing Power of Doing Good.* He dedicated his career to understanding volunteerism with an emphasis on how helping others can help one's own mental and physical health. However, I believe Luks's advice applies to optimizing volunteerism for both helper and recipient.

Here are eight of his ideas to achieve that goal:

- Help in person. When you can, try to meet and spend time with the people you are helping. This increases the connection between you and them. Autonomous activities such as writing a check or collecting clothing and food are important too, but the personal touch helps you both.
- Help often. According to Luks, the magic number is approximately two hours per week of volunteer work. Frequently helping in person builds bonds as the recipients see that they are important to you.
- Help strangers. Helping friends and family is important, but these are people that you "have to" help. Assisting strangers involves freely given acts, as opposed to stressful obligations, and likely are to be highly appreciated.
- Share commonality. Having something in common with the people you are helping increases impact. For example, if you are both victims of the same illness or hardship, such similarity increases empathy and social bonding.
- Work through an organization. A supportive organization that provides structure to your efforts is beneficial. This is because

you are more likely to stick with helping if you are involved in a formal program.

- Use your expertise. Being good at the kind of skills and expertise that the help requires will lead to an increased sense of contribution, self-determination, and genuine usefulness. And for the recipient, how would you like being helped by someone who didn't know what they were doing?
- Exert yourself. Assistance that requires exertion increases your involvement and attention. Interestingly, the exertion can cause increased levels of energy, not fatigue. And your hard work will be noticed and appreciated by those you help.
- Let go. It's crucial to do the best you can and then "let go" of results. Try to enjoy the social bonds that you have built and suppress expectations of the benefits that you expect to receive or give. This will reduce tension for everyone involved.

Luks believed that assisting others can produce what he called the "helper's high." This includes positive feelings, increased energy, and increased self-esteem. In the end, it's a win–win: helping others can foster emotional well-being for you and your recipients, so help others and you will benefit too.

Make Wise Interventions

∠ You wonder how to foster a sense of self-worth in others.

∠ You need some specific techniques for conducting wise interventions.

∠ You are looking for ways to make a positive impact in small, tactical ways.

Geoffrey Cohen, the professor of psychology at Stanford who developed the concept of "good situations" also recommends "wise interventions." He defines this as "interventions that nurture people's belonging and self-worth."

These interventions are brief (ten minutes), inexpensive, and targeted with the intention of long-term behavioral change. He explained the technique to me by citing a study in the Miami-Dade area where canvassers went door to door to discuss transgender rights. The interviews were structured in this way:

- Ask open-ended, thought-provoking questions, such as "What do you feel about transgender rights?" to foster discussion.
- Listen to people's answers and affirm the validity of their opinions to give them "voice."
- Insert "analogic perspective taking," which is the process of calling up a person's own experiences and emotions. For example, the canvassers said, "There's a lot of cases in which people experience the pain of being treated differently just because they're different. Can you think of a time in your life when you had that experience?"
- Listen to the shared story when the person was treated differently.
- Freeze the experience and lesson. "Given our conversation today, how has it affected your views of transgender rights? Has it changed you in any way? Do you think you'll support it more, support it less, or remain unchanged?"

Geoffrey summarized the results:

Six months later, they found that these people were much more sympathetic to transgender rights and actually more likely to take a stand against anti-transgender hate propaganda.

I think this is incredibly inspiring, and just goes against this wisdom that people don't change. People do change, but it takes the right kinds of keys.

Wise interventions involves transformative power because they serve as a reminder that people are capable of change, but it often requires the right blend of empathy, introspection, and connection.

By asking others the appropriate questions, listening to their responses, and encouraging them to reflect on their experiences, we can foster in them a sense of belonging and self-worth.

Over-Deliver

∠ You want to learn how to over-deliver in your work and personal life.

∠ You seek tangible examples of how to over-deliver.

∠ You want to know if good enough is "good enough."

In the summer of 2023, I purchased a takeout order from Ranch Milk Mexican Grill in Watsonville, California. The chef forgot to include the four shrimp tacos I ordered. The next time I visited a week later, I mentioned this, and the counter clerk instantly insisted on giving me four shrimp tacos based solely on my word.

When I told this story to two friends, they both told me that her decision was a common kind of reaction and therefore no big deal. I disagreed, so I checked with two experts: Andrew Zimmern (television host) and Roy Yamaguchi (creator of Roy's Restaurants).

Figure 8.3   Ranch Milk service station and restaurant in Watsonville, California, 2023.

(Source: Guy Kawasaki)

Here's what they said:

Andrew Zimmern: It's over-delivering in many ways, but more owners should empower their front-line workers to handle stuff exactly this way. I bet you will go back again and again to this place. That's real hospitality and more people should operate that way but few do.

Roy Yamaguchi: My initial reaction would be awesome, what great customer service. When an employee takes action and finds solutions to a problem this is priceless. Getting an okay sometimes from a manager doesn't produce the same feeling when it's done in an instant.

Don't get me wrong: it's wonderful when you or your organization over-delivers in big ways, such as an electric car that goes further than its official rating, but the little things are meaningful too.

Here are the basic concepts of how to over-deliver.

- Do more than expected. Educators are a good example of this. They spend their off-hours grading papers and preparing lessons. They buy supplies with their own money. In my book, teaching is a remarkable profession in and of itself.
- Trust people. This is what happened in my case of the missing tacos. The counter clerk trusted that I wasn't trying to scam her out of four tacos. Mathematically, the gain in positive karma, loyalty, and word-of-mouth reputation far outweighs the potential loss from being scammed out of four tacos.
- Be flexible. A fellow surfer passed away a few years ago. Twelve of us and his family gathered for a memorial brunch at a restaurant that was nearly empty. However, it refused to accommodate us. Just down the street at Cat and Cloud, the largest table was in the employees' only area, and the manager permitted us to use it. I didn't eat at that first restaurant for over a year.

All these methods have one thing in common: they make people feel valued. Exceeding expectations exemplifies generosity of time, effort, and trustworthiness. This is evidence of a remarkable and gracious person, and it can come across in the form of either grand or understated gestures.

I am a stickler for consistency, and every section in each chapter ends with a summary statement like the paragraph above. Except this one. This is because I wanted to verify that teachers generally over-deliver, so I posed the question to the remarkable Kelly Gibson, high school teacher in rural Oregon. Here is her answer:

> *For almost all teachers I know, going above and beyond is not just part of the job, not just part of a day but usually part of every hour of our work.*
>
> *Yes, we do buy extra supplies for our classrooms, we put in many extra hours, well beyond expectation, we give up time with our families, we work with students before and after school hours, but I would say one of the most important ways we demonstrate this quality is in our insistence on making connections to our students.*
>
> *Teachers inevitably care about every individual in their classrooms. We keep an eye on them when they seem sad. We celebrate with them when they seem happy. We attend their after-school events. We encourage them to do well in other classes, and we become part of their lives, as they become part of ours.*
>
> *And those connections often remain intact long after our students are no longer in our classrooms and are no longer our job.*

Change How You Keep Score

- ∠ You wonder how to measure your success in a meaningful way.
- ∠ You need some specific examples of how to be more impactful, fulfilled, and content.
- ∠ You want to develop the mindset of pursuing the act of difference making as the ultimate end goal.

What is important to a person is the test of grace. Over the course of interviewing hundreds of remarkable people, I came to the conclusion that they prioritize helping others over their own glory, and that's how they define "success."

For example, when I asked Jon M. Chu, film director, how he measures his success, he told me by the quality of roles actors in his films get in the future. Being remarkable means rising above basing your self-worth on money, power, or fame.

How you keep score says a lot about you, so here are some areas to examine to ensure you're on the right path:

- Impact. Sal Khan, creator of Khan Academy, told me he cares about how many kids he's helped educate around the world. Remarkable people keep score by how much they've improved the world, not how much money or power they've accumulated.
- Fulfillment. This means you love what you do, and you do what you love. Whatever the activity, it fills you with energy and provides reason for living. You feel like you've done something noble and good.
- Relationships. One measure of success is the quality of your relationships. Hopefully, you've brought joy into the lives of others, and they have brought joy into yours. In short, you loved and were loved.
- Growth. Over the course of your lifetime you can measure your success by how much knowledge and skills you've gained. This means that expanding your horizons is a satisfying thing. This can even apply to learning to surf.
- Resilience. You're probably successful if you can persevere in the face of challenges and failure. In other words, when you were tested, did you pass? And can you pass more tests in the future? If so, you can declare victory.
- Contentment. This means that you don't long for more of anything—except maybe time with your family and friends. Contentment indicates that you've realized what's truly important in life.

People who keep score this way are almost always gracious. If you keep score this way, you will become gracious too. The people who keep score with money, power, and fame are seldom gracious. They see everyone as a means to their end.

Your life comes down to your legacy, and how you keep score determines your legacy. I hope you made people's lives better. I hope the world is better for you having lived in it. These are the kind of legacies that matter and what remarkable people pursue.

Punch Up, Not Down

∠ You want to be more compassionate and understanding of others.

∠ You need help identifying and avoiding punching-down behavior.

∠ You want to lift others up, not tear them down.

Punching down involves belittling, criticizing, or attacking people who have less power, money, or social standing. In the United States, circa 2023, punching down usually occurs against marginalized people: white against Black, male against female, rich against poor, physically abled against physically challenged confrontations.

A remarkably dark example of punching down occurred in 2015 when Donald Trump, at the time the billionaire Republican candidate for the presidency of the United States, made fun of Serge Kovaleski, a reporter who has a disease called arthrogryposis.

Figure 8.4 *New York Times* **reporter Serge Kovaleski. He suffers from a disease that causes multiple joint contractures.**

(Source: Neilson Barnard/Getty Images)

Figure 8.5   Donald Trump mimicking Kovaleski in 2015.
(Source: © Richard Ellis/Zuma Press)

This ailment involves multiple joint contractures and deformities. Trump used wild, awkward arm movements to mock Kovaleski at a rally in Myrtle Beach, South Carolina, in 2015. Trump's desire to humiliate someone in order to get laughs was on full display. It is a perfect example of behavior unbecoming of a remarkable person.

In short, punching down is for assholes. It reflects a total lack of grace, class, and intelligence. However, punching up, done strategically, can be beneficial:

- Rally the troops. An act of defiance against a more powerful foe can supercharge employees and supporters.
- Raise money. Remember how Olivia Julianna used Matt Gaetz's attack to raise money for abortion rights?
- Send a message. Punching up can send a message that you're not going away quietly.

Here's an example of strategic punching up. In May 18, 2023, the students of New College of Florida held their own graduation ceremony to protest and punch up at the hostile takeover of the school by conservatives. They called their ceremony "On Our Terms."

Figure 8.6   Grace Sherman spreading her wings and graduating from New College of Florida at the "alternative commencement," May 2023.

(Source: © Douglas R. Clifford/Tampa Bay Times via ZUMA Press)

The next day, the school's official graduation featured Dr. Scott Atlas, an advisor to Donald Trump during the pandemic. It was interrupted by shouts of "Murderer," "Stop making it about you," and "Wrap it up."

Remarkable people do not punch down. Clueless, arrogant, insensitive assholes punch down. End of discussion. That said, remarkable people trying to make a difference use punching up in strategic ways.

Ask "How?"

∠ You want to be more understanding and empathetic of people who have different beliefs than you.

∠ You wonder how to have more productive conversations with people who disagree with you.

∠ You need help transcending argumentation and fostering connection when conversing with people who hold contrasting beliefs.

I learned this principle in my 2022 interview with Mark Labberton, the former president of Fuller Theological Seminary, which is an educational institution that equips students for leading and working in Christian organizations.

Our interview turned into a discussion of the mindset of evangelicals when they advocate behavior inconsistent with the teachings of Jesus Christ. Mark told me that when you're interacting with people you don't agree with, do not focus on *what* people believe nor *why* they believe it.

Instead, he recommended asking *how* they came to their beliefs. This perspective fosters greater understanding and maybe even empathy, rather than hostility:

> That question "How?" is really different than, "Why do you believe this?"
>
> "How" is a narrative, and almost all of our "whys" are undergirded by "hows." It's "How did you come to be convinced that that was true? How did you come to think in that way? How did you come to experience life in the way that you're describing that now requires the response that you're making? How did that actually unfold?"
>
> That question, "How?" can be an amazing tool in helping people who are not like each other find each other in a different way. If I'm sitting there and having somebody unload their story of how they came to hold that conviction, I'm suddenly in a really different place than I would be if we'd just been having debate.
>
> "Why" ends up creating often a defensiveness, but "How" creates an invitation, "I want to know you and I want to know your story."

With hindsight, back when I was a Macintosh evangelist at Apple, instead of asking what operating system a person used and why they were using it, I could have asked how they came to use MS-DOS or Windows. I would have been a better Macintosh evangelist had I known this back then.

There's still time so that you don't make the same mistake that I did.

Asking "how" promotes understanding and empathy. It helps you transcend argumentation when conversing with people who hold contrasting beliefs. This strategy not only helps you to connect on a deeper level, but also enables you to be a more effective influencer and leader in your own right.

Learn How to Apologize

∠ You want to learn how to give a good apology.

∠ You need help taking ownership for your actions and expressing empathy.

∠ You want to be a more remarkable person by doing what is necessary and expected of you.

It would be great if you never did anything incorrectly, inadequately, or insufficiently, but that's not how life works. The high road to being remarkable is paved with mistakes and failures, and a good apology goes a long way to correcting wrongs and to building relationships.

Lisa Leopold, my buddy from the Middlebury Institute of International Studies, is an expert in apologies because she taught a business communication course for international graduate students. Here are her four components:

- Say the words "I am sorry" or "I apologize" to start. Not phrases such as "I never intended," or "It was an accident." Just say you're sorry because the burden is on you to truly apologize.
- Specify what you did. Otherwise, people won't know what you're sorry about. At an extreme, are you sorry for getting caught or for what you did? Don't label it as a "mistake," "unfortunate," "bad luck," or "unintentional."
- Take ownership. Don't qualify your apology by saying, "If I offended or hurt," which implies that if you didn't offend or hurt anyone, you're not sorry. Take ownership. What's important is what the other person thinks, not you.

- Express empathy. Your apology should include an acknowledgment of the damage you caused, and you accomplish this by expressing empathy.

I asked Lisa to grade a few public apologies. Here are my favorite two reports. First is Mark Zuckerberg apologizing for a security breach in 2013 that exposed Facebook customer information:

We didn't take a broad enough view of our responsibility, and that was a big mistake. It was my mistake, and I'm sorry. I started Facebook, I run it, and I'm responsible for what happens here.

This is Lisa's analysis of Mark's apology:

Grade C−. The apology begins with the pronoun "we." If it is for an individual offense, the use of the pronoun "we" weakens responsibility. The word "mistake," even though it is a "big mistake," is nonetheless a weak way to characterize the offense.

In fact, not taking a "broad enough view of our responsibility" does not adequately acknowledge wrongdoing, because it is not really doing anything wrong per se, just not doing enough of something. There is an attempt at ownership with the words, "It was my mistake," and while "my" does claim responsibility, "mistake" weakens the depiction of the offense.

It is not clear whether "I'm sorry" is an expression of apology or regret, and those words are distanced from the naming of the transgression. He is stating the obvious with the expression, "I started Facebook, I run it," and that adds nothing of value to the apology.

It is good to say, "I'm responsible for. . ." as a way to claim ownership, but the choice of words for "what happens here" suggests that he may not have control over the company's operations.

Second, here is an apology from Paul Sherrell, a Tennessee state legislator who suggested hanging criminals from trees for death penalty sentences in 2023:

My exaggerated comments were intended to convey my belief that for the cruelest and most heinous crimes, a just society requires the death penalty in kind. Although a victim's family cannot be restored when an execution is carried out, a lesser punishment undermines the value we place on protecting life. My intention was to express my support of families who often wait decades for justice. I sincerely apologize to anyone who may have been hurt or offended.

This is Lisa's analysis of Paul's apology:

Grade D−. Most of this apology reads as a justification for his suggestion (as he expressed "intended" and "intention" twice in the statement).

There is absolutely no remorse. Calling his comments "exaggerated" hardly captures how offensive they are. The words "I sincerely apologize" are appropriate, but he does not apologize for the transgression but rather for others' (potential) feelings.

There is even a suggestion that there are no victims with the use of hedging in "anyone who may have been hurt or offended." The justification for the transgression, the lack of remorse, the suggestion that there may be no victims, the masking of the seriousness of the offense, and the apology issued only for the potential hurt (rather than the offense) render this apology pretty awful.

I would add one more recommendation about apologies. As much in life, when it comes to apologies, timing is everything. The longer you wait, the harder it is to apologize and the more damage the lack of an apology will do.

On the other hand, if you apologize too fast, then the victim can interpret your rush as an attempt to trivialize what happened and quickly move on. My advice is to wait for a moment of sufficient gravitas for your apology.

To summarize this discussion of apologies, which is probably more than you've ever wanted to read about the topic: 1) simply say "I'm sorry," 2) accept responsibility for your actions, 3) demonstrate compassion, and 4) choose the appropriate moment.

Ignore the Small Stuff

- ∠ You want to learn how to give people the benefit of the doubt.
- ∠ You wonder how to react to microaggressions in a way that is both productive and respectful.
- ∠ You want to learn how to worry about what matters.

You can learn as much about a person from what they ignore as from what they prioritize. And the more people ignore stuff, the more time and energy they have to devote to what is essential.

With all due respect to Socrates, John Locke, and Thomas Gray, all of whom are cited as possible sources of the saying "Ignorance is bliss," not knowing can be good, but the ability to ignore the small stuff is even better.

Here's a personal example. In 1994 I was living in San Francisco with my wife and baby boy. Our house was a block from the Presidio in an expensive, mostly white neighborhood.

One day I was outside our house trimming the bougainvillea plant, and an older, white woman came up to me and asked, "Do you do lawns too?" I retorted, "Because I'm Japanese, you assumed I'm the gardener, right?"

A few weeks later my father visited me, and I told him the story. I expected him to get agitated and annoyed that she assumed that his educated, author, former Apple executive son was the yardman.

Instead, he said, "Statistically, where you live, she was probably right, so don't get upset and make yourself crazy." Believe it or not, that was a pivotal moment in my life because it taught me not to look for trouble and to give people the benefit of the doubt.

Here are the principles of the "ignoring" superpower:

- Don't take things personally. The lady who asked me if I did lawns wasn't necessarily trying to belittle me. So if Apple has a policy that pisses you off, don't think that Tim Cook singled you out. He has no idea who you or I am.
- Don't worry about something you cannot do anything about. If you can't do anything about a situation, let it go. For example, the airline delayed your flight to de-ice your plane's wings. What will

Figure 8.7 The bougainvillea hedge where my yard care career began and ended.

(Source: Beth Kawasaki)

yelling at the employees at the gate accomplish? Plus, you'll be a lot more delayed if the plane crashes because of extra weight.

■ Give people the benefit of the doubt. Almost all the time, people are diligent, competent, and doing their job, so go through life assuming that people are good until proven bad. In fact, I'd give them two or three strikes before drawing any conclusions. The bougainvillea lady probably just wanted her lawn cut and wasn't intentionally being racist.

■ Check both sides of the story. You don't know what people are dealing with and what their perception of a situation is. Maybe the person taking a long time to back out of the parking space is coping with a death in her family. You never know. And someday you'll be in her shoes and be distracted and defocused.

Ignoring the small stuff can also be satisfying because you're in control and you know what's not getting to you, and it can be good for your reputation because counterattacking (and its temporary high) will not impress anyone.

But wait, there's more. I mentioned the story of my yardman-seeking neighbor in my 2022 interview with Frederick Joseph, the Black activist and author of *The Black Friend* and *Patriarchy Blues*. Much had happened by then in terms of race relations since the woman asked me if did lawns and my father told me to chill.

Here's what Frederick said I should have done:

> *In that specific situation, a real dialogue being had about "what you did was problematic X, Y, and Z, and you could say whatever you want, but if I were a white guy doing the exact same thing, I highly doubt that you would." That conversation might change her more than jumping down her throat.*

Which is to say that I could have taken the opportunity to explain that what she said could be construed as racist and demeaning. This would combine giving her the benefit of the doubt and using the encounter as an opportunity for enlightenment.

So much of life is uncontrollable. However, we can choose our reactions and responses. If you want to be remarkable, take the high road, give people the benefit of the doubt, and use each opportunity to foster greater understanding and communication. That is, don't do what I did . . .

By the way, read Frederick's *The Black Friend*. It is an extraordinary montage of remarkable sarcasm and zingers you should not miss.

Listen to My Parents

∠ You want to learn how to carry yourself with dignity and respect, even when no one is watching.

∠ You wonder how to be generous with your time, money, and resources, especially to those in need.

∠ You need help understanding the importance of leaving places cleaner than you found them.

And last but not least, let me provide three pieces of advice from my parents, Duke and Lucy Kawasaki. They are not poster or quote-graphic quality, but they have guided me nonetheless:

- Show. Some. Class. Don't lower your dignity or worth. Don't get drunk or stoned in public. Don't create a ruckus. Don't hassle people. Don't try to teach people a lesson. "Still waters run deep."
- Don't be a tight ass. Tip big—frontline and service workers are trying to survive. Don't split checks—alternate who pays instead. Don't negotiate just to exercise your power. Let people make a profit and a living.
- Leave everywhere cleaner than when you found it. My mother hammered this into me. I don't always meet her expectations (I had to say this in case my wife reads this book), but at least I am aware of the goal. That's a start . . . .

You will have numerous opportunities to make good decisions—often when no one is looking. The best option is often not the easiest one. Nevertheless, part of being remarkable is selecting the options that you can look back on with satisfaction.

Additional Resources

- Joseph, Frederick. *The Black Friend: On Being a Better White Person.*
- Kawasaki, Guy. *Wise Guy: Lessons from a Life.*
- Luks, Allan. *The Healing Power of Doing Good: The Health and Spiritual Benefits of Helping Others*
- Webster, Chris. *Confessions of a Chauffeur.*

9 | Turn and Burn

The best time to plant a tree was twenty years ago.
The second-best time is now.

—Chinese Proverb

Leave No Regrets Behind

∠ You want to learn from the regrets of others so that you can make better choices in your own life.

∠ You wonder what the most common regrets are and how you can avoid them.

∠ You want to live a more moral and compassionate life so that you have fewer regrets in the future.

Daniel Pink is an author, speaker, and host of the World Regret Project. The latter is a website where 19,000 people from 105 countries have revealed their regrets in life. His analysis of the results led to a book called *The Power of Regrets*.

We all have regrets—even remarkable people—so we can all learn from Daniel's findings to adjust our priorities. According to Daniel, the top four types of regrets are:

- Foundation regrets. *People around the world regret not exercising enough, not taking care of their bodies, not studying hard enough in school, not saving money—things where you didn't do the work, and as a consequence, your platform is a little wobbly.*
- Boldness regrets. *Overwhelmingly, in my research and in other research, people regret inactions way more than actions. They regret what they didn't do way more than what they did do. People regret not starting a business and staying in a lackluster job. I got huge numbers of people around the world regretting not asking someone else on a date.*
- Connection regrets. *Regrets where there was a relationship, or there should have been a relationship, and somehow it drifted apart. These connection regrets are the biggest category. Among the things I discovered in looking at these is that the way our relationships come apart, typically, is not dramatic. That is, we think that relationships come apart by some kind of blowout fight, and that's rarely the case. A lot of times they just drift, and drift.*
- Moral regrets. *I have hundreds of people who regret bullying kids at school when they were younger. I had a woman who broke into tears recounting the story of bullying a kid when she was eight years old, and she's in her fifties.*

According to Daniel, these regrets show us what we want out of life. His work underscores the importance of building a foundation by making wise choices, having the courage to take bold actions, nurturing and valuing relationships, and acting with morality and compassion. By acknowledging these common regrets, you can make a difference and live a remarkable life.

Heed Stacey's Creed

∠ You want to learn how to persevere through setbacks and achieve your goals.
∠ You seek inspiration from someone who has powered through disappointments.
∠ You need help finding your purpose and making a difference in the world.

After two years of pursuit, I was able to interview Stacey Abrams in June 2023. (One of my regrets is not going to be that I gave up on trying to get her on my podcast.) Stacey is a politician, political activist, entrepreneur, and author.

Her work in Georgia in 2020 to increase voter participation resulted in the election of two Democratic senators, and this prevented Republican control of the US Senate. These actions helped save democracy in the United States and prevent one giant step backwards for humanity.

One day she might be president, but she lost her first bid to become the governor of Georgia in 2018, and then she lost again in 2022. To paraphrase Senator Mitch McConnell, nevertheless Stacey persists.

Stacey was on a book tour in Santa Cruz, so we met at my house. Nothing would have made me happier than to interview *Governor* Abrams, but the fairy tale wasn't to be.

However, the silver lining is that her two losses in the governor's race allowed me to probe how she persevered despite setbacks, which is a valuable lesson for us all. So I asked her, "How do you keep going?

Figure 9.1 Stacey Abrams and I throwing shakas at my house after our June 2023 interview.

(Source: Madisun Nuismer)

How do you wake up every morning and still charge out the door?"
to which she responded:

> *I believe in three things. One, be curious. Ask questions, try to think about*
> *things, especially different ideas, and that's one of the reasons I write. It's*
> *why I start businesses. It's why I start organizations. It's why I'm engaged*
> *in politics. I am curious. We need to be curious about our world.*
>
> *Number two, solve problems. I am deeply discomforted by just knowing*
> *something's wrong and not doing something about it. So I believe in trying to*
> *solve problems. I try to fix things. I know I may not get it done, but I'm going to try.*
>
> *And then three. And most importantly, to me, my mission is to do good.*
> *If you know that there's something out there, try to do good. So it's three*
> *things I think every morning: be curious, solve problems, do good.*

The Gospel according to Stacey is the perfect ending to this book.
Her admonition to "be curious" is Growth; "solve problems" is Grit,
and "do good" is Grace. When all is said and done, this is what it takes
to be remarkable and make a difference.

Turn and Burn

∠You are done with reading and learning and want to start doing.

When I die, I hope you can say that I helped you make a difference. I am ending with my top ten tips for being remarkable because
we've covered so much material:

1. **Make the world a better place.** This is what remarkable people
   do. Money, fame, fortune, and followers are usually incidental.
   They are not the priority.
2. **Keep on growing.** Remarkable people don't stop learning.
   They are exploring, not boring. It doesn't occur to them that
   they have "arrived" or that they are "done."
3. **Do good shit.** These three little words define what makes a
   difference and what remarkable people do. They provide a

conceptual framework for what you want to accomplish with your life.

4. Plant lots of seeds. You have to plant many acorns to get just a few oaks. You never know which will take root, which will be eaten by the deer, and which will grow up strong and mighty.

5. Raise the tide. Life is not a zero-sum game if you're trying to make the world a better place. The rising tide floats all boats. And the falling tide brings down everyone.

6. Trust the dots. The only way to see how the dots connect is by looking backwards. There's no way to predict the ultimate outcome, so give yourself a break and keep trying.

7. Find your *ikigai*—that which gives your life meaning and purpose. It may take you years, and you may even transition from one to another.

8. Make yourself valuable and unique. When you do something that's needed and you are the best at it, you'll make a difference, and you're on your way to being remarkable.

9. Keep at it. To succeed you must stand up one more time than you fall down. Everyone will forget the number of times you failed if you succeed, and grit overcomes talent in the real world.

10. Take the high road. There's little traffic on the high road because only remarkable people go there. This means giving people the benefit of the doubt and believing people are good until proven bad.

Bonus: Make decisions right. In this rapidly changing world with limited data and unpredictability, right decisions are hard. Instead, make the best decision you can and then focus on making that decision right. Implementation trumps cogitation.

In surfing most of the time is spent gazing out to sea in search of waves. When a wave looks good, you turn and paddle for it—this is called "turning and burning." Now that you know what I know, it's time for you to turn, burn, and make that wave right because you won't catch 100% of the waves you don't paddle for.

Additional Resource

- Abrams, Stacey. *Our Time Is Now: Power, Purpose, and the Fight for a Fair America.*

Afterword

Some things need to be believed to be seen.

—Guy Kawasaki

Halim Flowers is an activist and artist. Starting at the age of sixteen, he served twenty-two years in prison for a murder he did not commit, nor aid and abet.

While in prison he became an artist, scholar, and author. Think of him as the next Jean-Michel Basquiat.

I asked him what it takes to actualize one's goals, since he was able to actualize many of his goals while in prison. This was his response:

A remarkable individual is someone who has committed to an outcome in spite of the odds or the circumstances. They revisit that goal every moment that they can. Even if it's not physically doing something, they're thinking about it. They're envisioning it.

They have the audacity to love themselves enough to constantly re-mark, re-put that mark on their sight, on their heart, on their soul, on their tongue, on their limbs, to work towards something that most people can't see. That's remarkable.

Halim Flowers with the Think Remarkable painting he created after our interview, November 2023.

(Source: Lauren McKinney)

List of Profiles

> Fame usually comes to those who are thinking about something else.
>
> —Oliver Wendell Holmes

My surfing buddy Karon Rohan tried to explain who I was to two other surfers as I was writing this book. She told them I had a podcast with guests like Jane Goodall, assuming that just mentioning Jane's name would establish my legitimacy.

It wasn't the case. They said they thought they heard of Jane Goodall but weren't sure who she was. After I regained consciousness, I recognized that I couldn't presume references to people were always understood, so we compiled this List of Profiles.

We've denoted the people who have been guests on the *Remarkable People* podcast. Through unintentional search optimization, we found that if you Google the person's name and add "remarkable people," you'll find the episode. For example, Google "David Aaker remarkable people" or "Stacey Abrams remarkable people."

Aaker, David. Professor emeritus at UC Berkeley's Haas School of Business. Considered the "father of branding." (Guest)

Abbott, Greg. Politician and attorney. 48th governor of Texas. Republican.

Abrams, Stacey. Politician and activist from Georgia. Prolific author of both fiction and nonfiction. Democrat. (Guest)

Adams, Cameron. Co-founder and chief product officer of Canva.

Altschuler, John. Television and film writer and producer. Co-creator of *Silicon Valley*.

Amendola, Joseph. Chef and mentor of Roy Yamaguchi. Author of *Understanding Baking: The Art and Science of Baking*.

Andrisse, Stanley. Endocrinologist and assistant professor at the Howard University College of Medicine. Author of *From Prison Cells to PhD: It Is Never Too Late to Do Good*. (Guest)

Angelou, Maya. Poet, memoirist, and civil rights activist. Author of *I Know Why the Caged Bird Sings*. Recipient of Grammy, Presidential Medal of Honor, and fifty honorary doctorates.

Archambeau, Shellye. Businesswoman and former CEO of MetricStream. Author of *Unapologetically Ambitious*. (Guest)

Atlas, Dr. Scott. Former White House COVID advisor (Trump administration; using the term "advisor" loosely), Stanford radiologist.

Atwater, Ann. Civil rights activist in North Carolina. Demonstrated that Black people and white people can collaborate for the common good.

Atwood, Margaret. Author of novels, poems, and essays, including *The Handmaid's Tale*. Awarded the Booker Prize twice and the Arthur C. Clarke Award. (Guest)

Balwani, Sunny. President and chief operating officer of Theranos. Convicted of wire fraud and conspiracy in 2022 and became prisoner 24965-111 in FCI Terminal Island prison.

Beck, Simone. French chef. Co-author of *Mastering the Art of French Cooking*.

Beethoven, Ludwig van. Composer and pianist.

Benioff, Marc. Co-founder, chairman, and CEO of Salesforce. Owner of *Time* magazine. Worked as summer intern for Guy at Apple. (Guest)

Berger, Jonah. Marketing professor at Wharton. Author of *Contagious* and *Invisible Influence*. (Guest)

Bertholle, Louisette. French chef. Co-author of *Mastering the Art of French Cooking*.

Bertish, Chris. Big-wave surfer, paddleboarder, adventurer, and motivational speaker. Crossed the Atlantic Ocean solo on a stand-up paddleboard. (Guest)

Bezos, Jeff. Founder and CEO of Amazon.

Biden, Joe. 46th US president. Democrat.

Boich, Mike. Technology entrepreneur and venture capitalist. First Macintosh software evangelist.

Bono. Irish singer-songwriter, activist, and philanthropist. Lead vocalist and primary lyricist of U2.

Boorstin, Daniel. Historian, professor, and the twelfth Librarian of Congress. Won the Pulitzer Prize for History for *The Americans: The Democratic Experience* in 1974.

Brown, Brené. Research professor at University of Houston and podcast host. Author of *Dare to Lead: Brave Work. Tough Conversations. Whole Hearts.*

Brown, Jim. Professional football player, actor, and activist. Considered the greatest running back in NFL history. Mentor of Ronnie Lott.

Bryar, Colin. Business advisor. Chief of staff for Jeff Bezos at Amazon. Author of *Working Backwards*. (Guest)

Cameron, Julia. Artist and teacher. Author of *The Artist's Way*. (Guest)

Cameron, Nigel. Imaginary inner critic of Julia Cameron.

Campbell-Wilson, Willa Alfreda. Activist, educator, and clinician focused on racial, feminist, and communication-disorder issues.

Carlson, Gretchen. Journalist, television personality at Fox, and women's rights activist. Helped take down Roger Ailes, then CEO of Fox. (Guest)

Chabris, Christopher. Professor and research psychologist. Co-author of *The Invisible Gorilla*.

Chance, Zoe. Professor at Yale School of Management, researcher, and climate philanthropist. Author of *Influence Is Your Superpower*. (Guest)

Chastain, Brandi. Soccer superstar. Two-time Olympic gold medalist and two-time FIFA Women's World Cup champion. (Guest)

Child, Julia. Chef and television personality. Co-author of *Mastering the Art of French Cooking*.

Child, Paul Cushing. Diplomat, author, and painter.

Chu, Jon M. Producer, screenwriter, and director of *Crazy Rich Asians*, *In the Heights*, and *Wicked*. (Guest)

Cialdini, Bob. Considered the "godfather of influence." Author of *Influence*. (Guest)

Clinton, Bill. 42nd US president from 1993 to 2001. Democrat.

Clow, Lee. Advertising creative director. Known for Apple's "1984" ad.

Cohen, Geoffrey. Professor of psychology and professor of education at Stanford University. Author of *Belonging*. (Guest)

Conway, John. Tesla owner, divorce lawyer, and surfer. Halved the spoils of countless Silicon Valley entrepreneurs. Lumpia assistant chef.

Conyers, Jonathan. Board member of the Brooklyn Debate League. Author of *I Wasn't Supposed to Be Here*. (Guest)

Cook, Tim. Chief executive officer of Apple. First openly gay CEO of a Fortune 500 company.

Cummings, Elijah. Politician and civil rights advocate who served in the US House of Representatives. Mentor of Leana Wen. Democrat.

Dalai Lama. Head monk of Tibetan Buddhism and considered a living Buddha.

Delbourg-Delphis, Maryléne. Tech entrepreneur, Silicon Valley philosopher, and thinker. Author of *Beyond Eureka!*

Dell, Michael. Billionaire businessman, founder and CEO of Dell Technologies.

DiColandrea, K.M. Educator and debate team coach. Selected as one of *New York Jewish Week's 36 to Watch* in 2022. (Guest)

Disney, Walt. Animator, film producer, and entrepreneur. Founder of the Walt Disney Company.

Duckworth, Angela. MacArthur Fellow. Professor of psychology at the University of Pennsylvania. Arguably, the "mother of grit," and author of *Grit*. (Guest)

Dutton, John. Fictional rancher played by Kevin Costner in the TV series *Yellowstone*.

Dweck, Carol. "Mother of the growth mindset." Professor of psychology at Stanford University. Author of *Mindset,* the second most influential book in Guy's life. (Guest)

Earhart, Amelia. Aviation pioneer. First woman to fly solo across Atlantic.

Ebert, Dave. Program director for the Pacific Shark Research Center and a research faculty member of the Moss Landing Marine Laboratories. Author of *Sharks of the World*. (Guest)

Einstein, Albert. Theoretical physicist who developed the theory of relativity.

Ellis, C.P. Former Ku Klux Klan "Exalted Grand Cyclops" who formed a friendship and partnership with Black activist Ann Atwater.

Fadell, Tony. Engineer and entrepreneur. Designed the iPod, iPhone, and Nest thermostat. Author of *Build*. (Guest)

Feigen, Marc A. Founder of Feigen Advisors LLC.

Flowers, Halim. Author, artist. Served 22 years in prison for a crime he didn't commit.

Fogg, BJ. Social scientist and research associate at Stanford University. Founder and director of the Stanford Behavior Design Lab. Author of *Tiny Habits*. (Guest)

Fonda, Jane. Actress, activist, and early adopter of Reebok aerobics shoes. Winner of two Academy Awards and seven Golden Globes.

Foster, Joe. Co-founder of Reebok. Author of *Shoemaker: The Untold Story of the British Family Firm That Became a Global Brand*. (Guest)

Frank, Anne. German-born diarist and victim of the Holocaust. Author of *The Diary of a Young Girl*.

Frey, Sarah. CEO and owner for Frey Farms. Snapping turtle tamer. Author of *The Growing Season*.

Frost, Maxwell. Politician, activist, and musician. First member of Generation Z to serve in the US Congress. Democrat.

Gabriel, Peter. Songwriter, musician, and record producer. Lead singer of the progressive rock band Genesis.

Gaetz, Matt. Body-shaming, grotesque US congressman from Florida. Republican.

Gandhi, Mahatma. Leader of the Indian independence movement against British rule.

Garcia, Hector. Software engineer. Author of *Ikigai*. (Guest)

Gates, Bill. Co-founder of Microsoft and philanthropist.

Gibson, Kelly. High school English teacher in Rogue River, Oregon. Gen Z whisperer for Guy. (Guest)

Ginsburg, Ruth Bader. US Supreme Court Justice from 1993 to 2020. Champion of women's rights and equality.

Girma, Haben. Deafblind disability rights advocate and the first deafblind person to graduate from Harvard Law School. Surfer. (Guest)

Gneezy, Uri. Professor of behavioral economics at the Rady School of Management at the University of California, San Diego. Author of *Mixed Signals*. (Guest)

Goldman, David. Director, critic, and founder of the National New Play Network at Stanford.

Goodall, Jane. Primatologist, anthropologist, and author. Founder of the Jane Goodall Institute. (Guest)

Gore, Al. Politician, environmentalist, and author. Former US vice president. His slideshow about climate change became the documentary *An Inconvenient Truth*. Democrat.

Graham, Bette Nesmith. Entrepreneur and inventor of Liquid Paper, the typewriter correction fluid.

Graham, Martha. Pioneer of modern dance.

Grandin, Temple. Animal scientist, autism spokesperson, advocate for people with autism, and author. (Guest)

Gray, Thomas. English poet of the Age of Enlightenment. Best known for *Elegy Written in a Country Churchyard*.

Gruner, Elisabeth Rose. English professor at the University of Richmond in Virginia. (Guest)

Harding, Wanda. Science, mathematics, and physics teacher. Senior mission manager at NASA. Oversaw the mission that sent the *Curiosity* rover to Mars. (Guest)

Harris, Kamala. US vice president, former US senator from California. Democrat.

Hastings, Reed. Entrepreneur and businessman. Co-founder, chairman, and former CEO of Netflix.

Hawking, Stephen. Theoretical physicist, cosmologist, and author who was diagnosed with amyotrophic lateral sclerosis (ALS) at the age of twenty-one.

Hoffman, Joanna. Early Apple marketing executive and member of the Macintosh team.

Hogg, David. Gun-control activist, survivor of the Parkland high school shooting.

Holmes, Elizabeth. Founder of Theranos. Convicted of fraud in 2022 and became prisoner 24965-111 at the Federal Prison Camp in Bryan, Texas.

Holmes, Oliver Wendell. Physician, poet, writer, and polymath. His writing is known for observations of the human condition.

Isaacson, Walter. Author, biographer of Steve Jobs, Einstein, da Vinci, Benjamin Franklin, Elon Musk, and others.

Jenkins, Michael. Partner at Kearney, a global management consulting firm.

Jesus. Son of God.

Jobs, Steve. Co-founder of Apple. Chairman and CEO of Pixar Animation Studios. Member of the Walt Disney Company's board of directors.

Jones, Norah. American singer-songwriter and jazz musician. Winner of eight Grammy Awards, including Best New Artist in 2003.

Joseph, Frederick. Activist and philanthropist. Author of *The Black Friend* and *Patriarchy Blues*. (Guest)

Joy, Bill. Tech pioneer and co-founder of Sun Microsystems.

Judge, Mike. Creator of *Beavis and Butt-Head* and co-creator of *King of the Hill* and *Silicon Valley*.

Julianna, Olivia. American political activist, abortion rights advocate, and ass-kicker from Texas. (Guest)

Kassalow, Jordan. Optometrist and social entrepreneur. Author of *Dare to Matter*.

Kawasaki, Duke. Father of Guy.

Kawasaki, Lucy. Mother of Guy.

Kawasaki, Nate. Santa Cruz graffiti artist and surfer. Son of Beth and Guy Kawasaki.

Kawasaki, Nohemi. Santa Cruz surfer, college student, and dog whisperer. Daughter of Beth and Guy Kawasaki.

Khan, Sal. Educator and founder of Khan Academy. Cousin of Nadia Khan, television performer and producer. (Guest)

Kovaleski, Serge. Investigative reporter for the *New York Times*. Best known for his coverage of the Eliot Spitzer prostitution scandal, the Iraq War, and the Trump administration.

Krinsky, David. Television writer and producer. Co-creator of *Silicon Valley*.

Labberton, Mark. Pastor and former president and CEO of Fuller Theological Seminary. (Guest)

Land, Edwin. Scientist, inventor, and co-founder of the Polaroid Corporation. Best known for inventing the Polaroid instant camera.

Langer, Ellen. American psychologist and author. Known for her work on the psychology of aging and mindfulness. (Guest)

Leakey, Louis. British paleoanthropologist who documented the origin of human beings in East Africa.

Lennon, John. Singer-songwriter, member of the Beatles.

Leopold, Lisa. Former program coordinator of English for Academic Purposes Program at Middlebury Institute of International Studies and former associate professor at Middlebury. (Guest)

Lévi-Strauss, Claude. Twentieth-century French anthropologist and one of the most influential thinkers on culture, religion, and social organization.

Lewis, C.S. Christian apologist and theologian. Author of the *Chronicles of Narnia* series.

Lightner, Candace. Founder of Mothers Against Drunk Driving (MADD).

Lindstrom, Martin. Branding expert, and business transformation expert. Author of *Buyology*. (Guest)

Locke, John. Philosopher and physician considered one of the most influential thinkers of the Enlightenment.

Lott, Ronnie. Professional football player. Four-time Super Bowl winner with the San Francisco 49ers. Awarded eight First-Team All-Pro selections, and ten Pro Bowl selections. (Guest)

Luks, Alan. Director emeritus of the Center for Nonprofit Leadership at Fordham University. Co-author of *The Healing Power of Doing Good*.

Lyons, Dan. Writer and journalist. Former senior editor at *Forbes* and a writer at *Newsweek*. Author of *STFU* and *Disrupted*. (Guest)

Lythcott-Haims, Julie. Speaker and activist. Former dean at Stanford University. Member of Palo Alto City Council. Author of *How to Raise an Adult*. (Guest)

Mandela, Nelson. Anti-apartheid leader and president of South Africa, 1994–1999.

Manson, Mark. Blogger. Author of *The Subtle Art of Not Giving a F*ck*. (Guest)

Mao, Chairman (full name: Mao Zedong). Founding father of the People's Republic of China and the leader of the Chinese Communist Party.

Martinez, Angel. Former chief marketing officer and executive vice president of Reebok International. Served as CEO of Keen, Decker Brands, and Rockport.

Martinez, Jacob. Director of Digital NEST in Watsonville, California.

Massey, Cade. Practice professor at Wharton School's Operations, Information and Decisions department and faculty co-director, Wharton People Analytics.

May-Treanor, Misty. Beach volleyball player, three-time Olympic gold medalist, teammate of Kerri Walsh Jennings.

McChrystal, Stanley A. Retired four-star general who served as the commander of US and NATO forces in Afghanistan, 2009–2010. Author of *Risk*. (Guest)

McConnell, Mitch. American politician, US Senate Minority Leader from Kentucky. Republican.

McNamara, Garrett. Total badass big-wave surfer. Set world record for largest wave surfed. (Guest)

Milkman, Katy. Professor of behavioral economics at Wharton. Author of *How to Change: The Science of Getting from Where You Are to Where You Want to Be*. (Guest)

Miranda, Lin-Manuel. Actor, singer, songwriter, and playwright. Winner of Grammy, Pulitzer Prize for Drama, and Tony Award. Works include *Hamilton* and *In the Heights*.

Moritz, Michael. Venture capitalist, philanthropist, author, and former journalist. Partner at Sequoia Capital, where he has invested in companies such as Google, LinkedIn, and PayPal.

Nalebuff, Barry. Business theorist, writer, and professor of management at Yale School of Management. Author of *Split the Pie*. (Guest)

Niño, Martha. Activist and student engagement community leader at Adobe. Author of *The Other Side*. (Guest)

Nuismer, Madisun. Producer of *Remarkable People* podcast. Co-author. Drop-in queen of Santa Cruz. First known case of "Long Bali."

O'Mara, Margaret. Historian and professor at the University of Washington. Author of *The Code*. (Guest)

Obama, Michelle. Former US first lady. Author and advocate for healthy living, education, and girls' empowerment.

Obrecht, Cliff. Co-founder and chief operating officer of Canva.

Overfelt, Brian. Surfer and photographer.

Panetta, Leon. Politician and statesman. Served as the director of the Central Intelligence Agency, secretary of defense, and a member of the US House of Representatives. Democrat. (Guest)

Pearlberg, Neil. Host of *Off the Lip* podcast. Intermediate-level standup paddle boarder in Santa Cruz, California.

Peet, Andrea Lytle. Activist and athlete. Completed marathons in all fifty states after being diagnosed with ALS. Co-founder of Team Drea Foundation. (Guest)

Perkins, Melanie. Co-founder and CEO of Canva. (Guest)

Peters, Tom. Business management consultant, speaker. Co-author, with Robert H. Waterman Jr., of *In Search of Excellence*. (Guest)

Picasso, Pablo. Painter, sculptor, printmaker, ceramicist, stage designer, poet, and playwright.

Pink, Daniel. Expert on motivation and human behavior. Author of *Drive*, *The Power of Regret,* and *To Sell Is Human*. (Guest)

Pinker, Steven. Cognitive psychologist, psycholinguist, and professor. Author of *Enlightenment Now*. (Guest)

Price, Catherine. American journalist. Author of *How to Break Up with Your Phone*. (Guest)

Rober, Mark. Inventor, STEM evangelist, and autism activist. Worked at NASA on the design of the *Curiosity* rover. Creator of wildly popular educational science videos on YouTube. (Guest)

Roberson, Joseph. CEO and managing partner at the California Ear Institute. Faculty member and former chief of Otology,

Neurology Skull Base Surgery at Stanford University. He literally opened up Guy's head.

Robinson, Ken. Author, speaker, and education evangelist who advocated for a more creative and inclusive approach to education. (Guest)

Rohan, Karon. United pilot and break-dominating surfer.

Rometty, Ginni. First female CEO of IBM. Advocate for diversity and inclusion in the tech industry. (Guest)

Rossman, Alain. Third software evangelist of Macintosh Division. Founder of nine tech companies.

Rubin, Gretchen. Host of *Happier* podcast. Author of *The Happiness Project* and *Life in Five Senses*. (Guest)

Rubin, Rick. Record producer, co-founder of Def Jam Recordings. Author of *The Creative Act: A Way of Being*.

Sanders, Bernie. American politician and activist serving as the senior US senator from Vermont. Independent.

Sasson, Steven. Electrical engineer who invented the first digital camera in 1975. Member of the National Inventors Hall of Fame.

Sawyer, Katina. Associate professor of management and organizations at the Eller College of Management at the University of Arizona.

Shultz, George. Economist, statesman, and diplomat. US secretary of state under President Reagan. Board member of Theranos.

Shultz, Tyler. Whistleblower who exposed the fraud at Theranos, the blood-testing startup of Elizabeth Holmes and Sunny Balwani. Grandson of George Shultz. (Guest)

Scott, MacKenzie. Philanthropist and ex-wife of Jeff Bezos. Executive director of Bystander Revolution. Author of *The Testing of Luther Albright*.

Sherman, Grace. 2023 graduate of New College of Florida.

Sherrell, Paul. Member of the Tennessee House of Representatives. Republican.

Simons, Daniel. Professor at the University of Chicago. Famous for the *Invisible Gorilla* video. Author of *Nobody's Fool*. (Guest)

Sivers, Derek. Musician, circus ringleader, and founder of CD Baby. Author of *Anything You Want*. (Guest)

Socrates. Greek philosopher considered one of the founders of Western philosophy.

Spielberg, Steven. Filmmaker and director of *Jaws*, *E. T. the Extra-Terrestrial*, and *Schindler's List*. Three Academy Awards, twelve Prime-time Emmy's, and nine Golden Globe Awards.

Steinem, Gloria. Feminist icon and journalist. Co-founder of *Ms.* magazine. Mentor of Jamia Wilson.

Suskind, Dana. Pediatrician, author, and founder and co-director of the TMW Center for Early Learning + Public Health at the University of Chicago. (Guest)

Takei, George. Iconic actor (helmsman Hikaru Sulu on Star Trek!) and LGBTQ+ rights activist.

Tandon, Chandrika. First Indian-American female partner at McKinsey and Company, Grammy-nominated musician, and board member of Lincoln Center for Performing Arts. (Guest)

Thompson, Nancy. Founder of MAGA. No, not that MAGA . . . this MAGA: Mothers Against Greg Abbott.

Thoroughgood, Christian. Assistant professor of management at the J. Mack Robinson College of Business, Georgia State University.

Thunberg, Greta. Swedish environmental activist. Initially known for her school strike for climate change.

Tomson, Shaun. Professional surfer who won the 1977 World Surfing Championship. Author of *Surfer and the Sage*. (Guest)

Trounce, Craig. Nordstrom employee who gave a customer a refund for tires even though the tires were bought from a former tenant of the building.

Trump, Donald. 45th US president. One term, two impeachments, four indictments, and 91 charges as of 2023. Republican.

Ueland, Brenda. Journalist and teacher. Author of *If You Want to Write*—the most influential book in Guy's life.

Ury, William. Academic anthropologist, and negotiation expert. Co-founder of the Harvard Program on Negotiation. Co-author of *Getting to Yes*.

Van Doren, Paul. Co-founder of Vans. Shaped the world of skate-boarding and youth culture with innovative footwear. Author of *Authentic*.

Vann, Michael G. Professor of history at California State University, Sacramento. Author of *The Great Hanoi Rat Hunt*.

Voltaire. Enlightenment writer, historian, and philosopher. Famous for criticism of Christianity and support of free speech and separation of church and state.

Walsh Jennings, Kerri. Professional beach volleyball player. Winner of three Olympic gold medals and one Olympic bronze medal. (Guest)

Ward, William Arthur. Inspirational author and thinker. His column, *Pertinent Proverbs*, was published by the *Fort Worth Star-Telegram*.

Warendh, Anton. Chief operating officer, Feigen Advisors LLC.

Webster, Chris. Limousine driver in Silicon Valley whose funeral Carol Dweck attended. Author of *Confessions of a Chauffeur*.

Webster, Jennica. Director of Marquette University's Institute for Women's Leadership and an associate professor in the Department of Management.

Wen, Leana. Physician, public health expert, and columnist for the *Washington Post*. Commissioner of the Baltimore City Health Department. (Guest)

Widman-Levy, Ronit. Executive producer of TEDx Palo Alto and director of the Israel Museum Council of the Bay Area.

Willis, Raquel. Transgender rights activist and writer. Author of *The Risk It Takes to Bloom*. (Guest)

Wilson, Jamia. Feminist activist and editor. Former director and publisher of the Feminist Press at City University of New York. Author of *Together We Rise*. (Guest)

Wineburg, Sam. Professor emeritus of education at Stanford and history and founder of Stanford History Education Group. Author of *Verified*. (Guest)

Winfrey, Oprah. Talk show host, actress, producer, author, and philanthropist.

Wolfram, Stephen. Computer scientist, theoretical physicist, author, and entrepreneur. Founder of Wolfram Mathematica and WolframAlpha. Youngest person to be named a MacArthur Fellow. (Guest)

Wozniak, Steve. Co-founder of Apple. Segway polo player. (Guest)

Yamaguchi, Kristi. Competitive figure skater, author, speaker, activist, and dancer. Winner of figure-skating gold medal at the 1992 Winter Olympics. Winner of *Dancing with the Stars* in 2008. (Guest)

Yamaguchi, Roy. Pioneer of Hawaiian fusion cuisine. Founder of Roy's Restaurants, a chain of restaurants with locations around the world. (Guest)

Yousafzai, Malala. Pakistani activist for female education and the youngest Nobel Prize laureate.

Zimmern, Andrew. Chef, television personality, and food writer. Host of *Bizarre Foods with Andrew Zimmern*. (Guest)

Zuckerberg, Mark. Co-founder, chairman, and CEO of Meta.

List of Podcast Guests

The wise man doesn't give the right answers; he poses the right questions.

—Claude Lévi-Strauss

David Aaker, Jennifer Aaker, Stacey Abrams, Jason Acuna, David Ambroz, Stanley Andrisse, Sinan Aral, Audrey Arbeeny, Shellye Archambeau, Margaret Atwood, Suzy Batiz, Maxine Bedat, Marc Benioff, Richard Benoit, Jonah Berger, Melissa Bernstein, Chris Bertish, John Biewen, Gabrielle Blair, Ken Blanchard, Steve Blank, Jonah Boaler, Tiffani Bova, Colin Bryar, Jonah Burger, Susan Cain, Julia Cameron, Gretchen Carlson, Steve Case, Zoe Chance, Gretchen Chapman, Brandi Chastain, Robert Chesnut, Jon M. Chu, Dolly Chugh, Bob Cialdini, Shane Claiborne, Dorie Clark, Geoff Cohen, Cecelia Conrad, Jonathan Conyers, Adam Curry, Doug DeMuro, Erica Dhawan, Rebecca DuBois, Angela Duckworth, John Lee Dumas, Carol Dweck, Esther Dyson, Dave Ebert, Amy Edmondson, Kurt Eichenwald, Pamela Ellis, Amy Errett, Dave Evans, Tony Fadell, Keith Ferrazzi, Tim Ferriss, Kathryn Finney, Ayelet Fishbach, Halim Flowers, Pat Flynn, BJ Fogg, Joe Foster, Latanya Mapp Frett, Sarah Frey, Valerie Fridland, Juliet Funt, Scott

Galloway, Héctor Garcia, Caleb Gardner, Henry Gee, Nancy Gianni, Kelly Gibson, Dario Gil, Haben Girma, Uri Gneezy, Seth Godin, Kara Goldin, Marshall Goldsmith, Jane Goodall, Sarah Stein Greenberg, Elisabeth Gruner, Mauro Guillén, Wanda Harding, Mehdi Hasan, Fran Hauser, David Haussler, Jeff Hawkins, Pamela Hawley, Cassie Holmes, Hugh Howey, Arianna Huffington, Michael Hyatt, David Ige, iJustine, Emma Isaacs, Barbara Jenkins, Luuvia Ajayi Jones, Frederick Joseph, Olivia Julianna, Nikhil Kamath, Jodi Kantor, Cody Keenan, Patrice Keet, Tim Kendall, Dave and Doug Kenricks, Jennifer Kerns, Sal Khan, Jerome Kim, Kim Komando, Lauren Kunze, Min Kym, Mark Labberton, Melissa LaHommedieu, Ellen Langer, Lisa Leopold, Jacqui Lewis, Neil A. Lewis Jr., Dominic Lieven, Jennifer Lim, Martin Lindstrom, John List, Taylor Lorenz, Ronnie Lott, Dan Lyons, Julie Lythcott Haims, Katherine Maher, Mark Manson, Temple Maslach, Christina Maslach, Renée Mauborgne, Stan McChrystal, Gladys McGarey, Syd and Shea McGee, Jane McGonigal, Garrett McNamara, Chris Messina, Katy Milkman, Karen Mullarkey, Vivek Murthy, Barry Nalebuff, Sheila Nazarian, Martha Niño, Randy Nonenberg, Don Norman, Margaret O'Mara, Paul Oyer, Julie Packard, Nicole Paiement, Leon Panetta, Abraham Paskowitz, Josh Peck, Torbjørn Pedersen, Andrea Lytle Peet, Melanie Perkins, Tom Peters, Daniel Pink, Steven Pinker, Catherine Price, Deepa Purushothaman, Stephen Pyne, Anne Rimoin, Mark Rober, Ken Robinson, Rebecca Rolland, Gloria Romero, Ginni Rometty, Robert Rosenberg, Gretchen Rubin, Peter Sagal, Patti Sanchez, Jeremy Sanford, Ted Scambos, Antoinette Schoar, Mark Schulman, Dionne Searcy, Tyler Shultz, Jerry Silver, Daniel Simons, Mike Sinyard, Derek Sivers, Rock Smolan, Martha Stewart, Dana Suskind, Chandrika Tandon, Doris Taylor, Paul Theroux, Shaun Tomson, Neil deGrasse Tyson, Gary Vaynerchuk, Jessica Wade, Jeanne Wakatsuki, Robert Waldinger, Kerri Walsh Jennings, Jim Weber, Tina Wells, Leana Wen, Alden Wicker, Raquel Willis, Jamia Wilson, Chip Wilson, Sam Wineburg, Dave Winer, Esther Wojcicki, Stephen Wolfram, Steve Wozniak, Olympia Yager, Roy Yamaguchi, Kristi Yamaguchi, Andrew Yang, Linda Zhang, Phil Zimbardo, and Andrew Zimmern.

Mahalo

Feeling gratitude and not expressing it is like wrapping a present and not giving it.

—William Arthur Ward

People

I could make the case that the Acknowledgments, or "Mahalo" in this case, is the first thing you should read in a book. The amount of testing, editing, and cogitating that goes into a book is often unseen and unappreciated.

Not in my book. Here are the people who helped us conceptualize, research, write, edit, and produce *Think Remarkable*.

Kelly Gibson. I happened to read a story in *Wired* about the impact of ChatGPT on high school education. The star of this article was Kelly Gibson of Rogue River, Oregon. What she had to say so impressed me that I had her as a guest on my podcast. And the goodness continued as she helped me make this book relevant to Gen Z in ways I couldn't have done without her.

Lisa Leopold. I have written sixteen books. Thousands of people have read drafts and hundreds have offered me feedback. Lisa is the best tester I have ever encountered. Her eye for detail and her logical thinking are remarkable. And she is an expert in the art of apologizing.

This is a group of people whom I forced to read multiple drafts and consider dozens of titles, subtitles, and covers. They did so with great enthusiasm, insightfulness, and care: John "Jian" Conway (he came up with the book's title), Joana "Zinc Face" Mana, Mark "the Dentist" Nishimura, "Uncle" Troy Obero, and Cynthea "Lady Bing" Thomas.

Not far behind them was the contribution of Valeria Fridland. And then there's Mustafa Ammar, Chip Bell, Nadja Conway, Tim Cottrell, Anthony Detro, Michael Dittmar, Lauren Enz, Neenz Faleafine, Kimber Falkinburg, Kathryn Henkens, Erin Holt, Christy Hutton, Beth Kawasaki, Nic Kawasaki, Nohemi Kawasaki, Sakura Kawasaki, Stuart Lord, Jim Lyons, Luis Magana, Bruna Martinuzzi, Bill Meade, Alexis Nishimura, Tessa Nuismer, Deborah Pagnota, Alison Parks, Emily Ann Pillari, George Pillari, Josh Reppun, Melissa Richards, Karon Rohan, Liam Rohan, Eric Schneider, Dan Simons, Craig Stein, Ruth Stevens, Jason Szolomayer, Carlos Thompson, and Danielle "Hang Ten" West.

In the middle of the summer of 2023, my publishing connections evaporated, and I was back to square one à la a first-time book author. Then out of the blue, Leah Zarra sent me an email inquiring about my interest in writing a book for Wiley. Without Leah, this book might not exist.

Without Leah and the other remarkable people at Wiley—namely, Simon Eckley, Michael Friedberg, Amy Handy, Julie Kerr, Amy Laudicano, Gabriela Mancuso, Jeanenne Ray, Deborah Schindlar, Suganya Selvaraj, and Shannon Vargo—this book wouldn't be as good. And a special callout to Chris Wallace for the remarkable cover. My thanks to them all.

Though some authors hide the fact that they use "artificial intelligence," we have no such qualms. We used Bard, Claude, ChatGPT, and Quillbot. There is no doubt in our minds that they helped make it better.

There are several products that make the Remarkable People podcast possible, which in turn made this book possible: Descript, Heil, Rev, Rode, and SquadCast. Members of the Remarkable People podcast team include Shannon Hernandez, Alexis Nishimura, Jeff Sieh, and Fallon Yates.

Places

The distractions in my home are too alluring for me to write there. Thus, I often work in coffee and food establishments. Here's a list of the places where I worked on *Think Remarkable.* Whoa, I had no idea I worked in so many places until I compiled it!

11th Hour Coffee (Santa Cruz), Atherton Library (Atherton), Betty's Burgers (Santa Cruz and Aptos), Bittersweet Bistro (Aptos), The Butter House (Seaside), Café La Tartine (Redwood City), Cafe Sparrow (Aptos), California Café (Watsonville), Cat and Cloud (Aptos and Capitola), Coffeebar (Menlo Park), Coffeetopia (Santa Cruz), Craft (Watsonville), Dean (Goleta), Dune Coffee Roasters (Santa Barbara), Foodland (Honolulu), Gino's Sicilian Express (Santa Barbara), The Hideout (Aptos), Joe's Café (Santa Barbara), Kabuki Hotel (San Francisco), La Vie (Honolulu), Lighthouse Coffee (Santa Barbara), Lulu Carpenter's (Santa Cruz), Mademoiselle Colette (Redwood City), Mr. Toots (Capitola), Olive Garden (Capitola), Orchard Valley Coffee (Campbell), Peets (Capitola), Quiora (Honolulu), Ranch Milk (Watsonville), Santa Barbara Public Market (Santa Barbara), Santa Cruz Public Library (Live Oaks and Capitola), Scarlet Begonia (Santa Barbara), Stacks (Menlo Park and Campbell), Starbucks (Capitola), Suda (Santa Cruz), Sunrise Café (Aptos), Walnut Café (Santa Cruz), Watsonville Public Library (Watsonville), Zizzo's Coffeehouse (Capitola).

About the Authors

Guy Kawasaki is the chief evangelist of Canva and host of the *Remarkable People* podcast. He was the chief evangelist of Apple, trustee of the Wikimedia Foundation, Mercedes-Benz brand ambassador, and special assistant to the Motorola Division of Google. Kawasaki has a BA from Stanford University, an MBA from UCLA, and an honorary doctorate from Babson College. He lives in Watsonville, California.

Madisun Nuismer is the producer of the *Remarkable People* podcast. Nuismer has a BA in public health from the University of Nebraska at Omaha. She also attended the Institute of Integrative Nutrition and is a certified holistic health coach. She lives in Santa Cruz, California.

Index

205